THE
PICNIC
COOKBOOK

ANNIE BELL

Photography by Jonathan Bell

Kyle Books

First published in Great Britain in 2012 by
Kyle Books
an imprint of Kyle Cathie Limited
23, Howland Street
London W1T 4AY
general.enquiries@kylebooks.com
www.kylebooks.com

ISBN: 978 0 85783 024 1

A CIP catalogue record for this title is available from the British Library

Annie Bell is hereby identified as the author of this work in accordance with Section 77 of the Copyright, Designs and Patents Act 1988

Text © Annie Bell 2012
Photographs © Jonathan Bell 2012
Design © Kyle Books 2012

Editor: Vicky Orchard
Design: Jenny Semple
Photography: Jonathan Bell
Food and Props Styling: Annie Bell
Production: Gemma John and Nic Jones

Colour reproduction by ALTA London
Printed and bound by Toppan Leefung Printing Ltd in China

ACKNOWLEDGEMENTS Another summer of fun spent out of doors, made possible by the many people who helped to make *The Picnic Cookbook* happen. With many thanks firstly to my agent Lizzy Kremer at David Higham, my sounding block, for her advice and for being there. To Kyle for all her support and giving us the opportunity. To Vicky Orchard, Editor, for calmly steering the idea from conception to publication. Nikki Sims for copy editing the book. Jenny Semple for the clarity of her design. Salima Hirani for proof-reading the manuscript. Vanessa Bird for her index. Julia Barder, as Sales and Marketing Director. Victoria Scales, for publicity. Lastly to my favourite companion on any picnic, my husband Jonnie, for his enthusiasm and his charming pictures and snaps. And to our long-suffering son Louis, his friends and our friends and relations, who gamely got into the picnic spirit and joined us on many locations.

CONTENTS

GREAT LOCATION, GREAT FOOD

'Where shall we meet for lunch?'

are six small words that send me into a flat spin. Finding good food is one thing, finding a great location another. Never one to embrace the mundane, my ideal is most likely either to be on the seventh floor of a building with panoramic views of the capital and revolve, or it's in the centre of a garden of Eden gently lit by uplighters concealed in the flowering Bouganvilleas surrounding our table, where we can dine to the backing vocals of cicadas.

In my dreams. Which is why I adore going on picnics. Before we get to the food (and fear not you have 170 pages following this musing on nothing else), picnics are about place. It is the magic seasoning and surprise, the unpredictability that leads to having fun, which makes them potentially some of the most memorable dining experiences. It is only once you have dreamt up the setting and designed the stage that you can actually start to plan what you are going to eat. If I think back over the picnics I have been on, they are mapped out in my memory as a series of postcards of where we have eaten. The windswept beach with its white sand and piercing blue sky where we sheltered from the elements between boulders encrusted with barnacles and draped with seaweed. Or the Springtime meadow of wild flowers when the tallest person in the party played St Christopher by carrying the faint-hearted across the shallow mountain stream that stood in the way. But there are city postcards too, the bench of a zoo in Bangkok and the shade of an orange tree in Seville, it's a great way of exploring the delis, food shops and markets of any place you happen to be visiting in the world.

Yet so often I find myself reading about picnics that go wrong. How can a picnic go wrong? Well I sort of know what you mean. I am thinking back to when, as impoverished students my husband and I went to Paris for a few days. The first picnic opportunity provided itself on the deck of a ferry across the English Channel, which to our unworldly innocence could have been the port side of a cruise ship for all its glamour. Well, we sat and sunned ourselves with our gin and tonics and egg mayonnaise rolls, as our conversation was drowned out by the vibrating hum of the engine room. So far, so romantic.

Arriving in Paris, having taken in the Centre Pompidou we went in search of a boutique hotel, which we had chosen for its proximity to a lively street market selling the sort of French food that had lured us in the first place. We downed our luggage and shopped for a picnic that we could eat in the Tuileries Garden, and then it started raining, and raining. The obvious tack was to retreat to our hotel room, which we hadn't actually inspected at that point, but it seems George Orwell had been there before us in *Down and Out in Paris and London*: the 'narrow street, a ravine of tall, leprous houses lurching towards one another in queer attitudes' and 'the walls were as thin as matchwood, and to hide the cracks they had been covered with layer after layer of pink paper, which had come loose'. Except that ours was nicotine brown. As I unwrapped our surprise package of cheeses the exchange with the vendeuse in the market floated back, 'Vous voulez le chevre bien fort?' 'Mais oui', I had replied as our picnic took on ever more profound Orwellian dimensions and the pervading scent of rank, mature goat's cheeses filled the damp room with its low rafters. But you

What's the plan?

know what, given the distance in years, I now look back on it fondly.

When it comes to picnics I am a glass half-full person. Admittedly I had to give goat's cheese a rest for a while, but these days nicotine-stained wallpaper doesn't come into it, my mind wanders to blue skies, an ambient breeze and the shade of a tree, a rug on which to sprawl, laughter, relaxation, and great food. In short, lunch or dinner in the location of your dreams or the dining room of your choosing.

Perhaps most of all I love picnics for their accessibility. They are a great leveller: they are open to anyone and everyone. You don't even have to do all the work yourself, the best in spirit are the sum of the parts where everyone brings something along and you all feast together. There is a delicious innocence about the whole experience, from the enthusiasm of plotting and planning where to go, what to pack, what to eat, what to do when you get there and who to go with. It's an adventure.

While we may not be able to control the elements, even the simplest of picnics benefit from planning. Perhaps the main faux pas is to assume that it is about grab a rug, a baguette and a few cold meats and go. What we can do, is maximise the chances of a picnic's success with a little forethought. Make sure that we have the requisite coldbags if it's a hot day, and remember to put the freezer blocks in the ice compartment the night before. And to pack the corkscrew, of course; on principle, I won't take a screw-top bottle on a picnic, which would ruin the challenge of not forgetting it.

And in addition, there are a few tips that as a veteran picnicker I feel make a difference. Taking two rugs, or more, instead of assuming that all five of you can comfortably lounge on one rug, with lunch for company. The average picnic rug is probably the size of a double bed, so work on the basis that one is bliss, two is cosy but three is definitely a crowd. And why not give lunch its very own rug or cloth, which does away with the hazard of sitting on it?

What shall we eat?

At last we come to the essential issue, of what to eat. While there may be different types of picnic, they are all rustic affairs at heart that involve getting down and dirty in the literal sense, and as such the call is for relaxed and bohemian cooking. If you can't imagine eating it lying down it probably doesn't fit. If it is a particularly special or slightly more formal picnic, you might want to extend this to include knives and forks, or even a trestle table, a cloth and chairs, but the food itself still needs to be casual. So even though what follows attempts to cover every picnic scenario, there is only one style of food, because only one style works.

As to type of picnic, broadly speaking there are three scenarios into which most will fall. First off there are spontaneous last-minute picnics. Next up from that are communal get-togethers, and more ambitiously special occasion fine-dining ones. Depending on which category your picnic is likely to fall into, which in turn will come with its own set of practical considerations, this will suggest the best menu. But all of what follows is designed to be simple, not least because I find it is easy to get carried away when planning picnics.

The walls of my home have been removed and therefore I can invite as many people as I choose. I am no longer worried about whether I have enough space at the table. Enough plates? No problem, we can take paper ones, and likewise glasses; and no need for cutlery because I'll plan for things that can be eaten with fingers. Suddenly what started out as a modest gathering is a party. But this is one of the great plusses, it's the spontaneity that makes them the occasions that they are.

LET'S GO
This is the seriously quick option. You can shop cleverly for lovely breads, cold cuts and cheeses, a few pickles, a bag of salad leaves and punnet of tomatoes and go. This kind of food involves the

minimum of preparation, and makes for one of the easiest types of picnic. So, every chapter starts with suggestions for instant ideas, goodies to buy in or that require the simplest possible attention before you leave.

For instance, you can whisk up a salad dressing using a couple of ingredients, and take a bunch of watercress or bag of lamb's lettuce; buy some ready-made dips, such as hummus and tzatziki, but give them a little twist at home and put them in a slightly more alluring container than their plastic supermarket tub. There are lots of ideas for puds, too, marriages of ingredients that will bring out the best in each other, whether that is pears with Manchego, or dates with some gooey Gorgonzola.

PASS IT ROUND
On from the instant picnic in terms of ease are those finger-foods that can be handed round, no cutlery called for, which is the demand of most

communal get-togethers be it a sports day, street party or a big birthday – occasions when everyone brings a plate or two of something. This tends to take a little more time in the kitchen, but at least it is all said and done in advance. This could be anything from chicken thighs roasted with lemon and za'atar, to Little Gem leaves filled with egg mayonnaise and strips of anchovy, or slices of Spanish tortilla, some cherry tomato and Parmesan tarts, finishing off with a decadent chocolate cake.

FINE DINING

Lastly there are the more ambitious types of picnic that involve plates, knives and forks. And there are occasions when this is the call, that opera or 'fête champêtre' when it is good to have some ideas up your sleeve. A plate of gravadlax with salad, a rack of lamb that can be sliced into delicate pink chops alongside a potato salad. When you do manage to pull it off, it can be completely magical, a glass of chilled Champagne as the sun disappears and solar lanterns hung in the trees start to glow.

MIX AND MATCH

In reality, a lot of the time, what suits will end up being a melange of all three types of picnic. Probably my favourite opportune weekend picnic, waking up on a beautiful summer morning with nothing planned, is to roast a chicken, buy a loaf of sourdough and some peppery green leaves and different tomatoes on the vine. Whisk your chicken wrapped in foil from oven to rug, where still slightly warm an hour or two later you can hack it into rustic slivers using a folding knife, and dip the bread and salad leaves in the juices. But just as simple, you could buy in some salami and roast ham, but make a lovely tomato salad or tabbouleh to go with them – in short, there are all sorts of halfway houses where you're not going to the trouble of preparing every dish, but cooking or preparing just one offering will give the picnic heart and soul over and above if you had bought absolutely everything ready-made.

Will it, Won't it Rain?

BEFORE

Typical. No sooner had I planned for a picnic this weekend and invited everyone, but they announced a 'break' in the fine September weather. As a consequence I have been glued to the local weather forecast for the last few days. On Wednesday they predicted 'heavy rain', on Thursday they down-graded it to 'light rain', and on Friday they upped it back up to 'heavy rain' adding in 'gusting winds'. Today? 'Light rain' apparently, so who knows?

But the plan is, we all meet in the park by the cedars and the statues, where we have a lovely lunch of roast ham and chicken, hummus, guacamole, slow-roast tomatoes and grilled broccoli, salt caramel millionaire's shortbread, polka dot cookies, blueberries and figs, all washed down with ginger beer, pink lemonade, pomegranate juice and cider, before playing a competitive round of volleyball. It is going to have to rain very hard before I cancel.

AFTER

I must have done something good in my life (a long, long time ago) because the rain never appeared. Or as a friend put it, 'How much did you pay and to whom?'. After all that fretting, the weather was lovely, sunny, ambient and autumnal, pretty much perfect in fact. I didn't even forget anything. The only hitch, was that when we laid our roast chicken still hot from the oven, down on the rug, it sparked the equivalent of the twilight barking of *101 Dalmations*, as word spread through the local canine population that dinner was served, and within minutes there were pooches flying at us from every direction. That aside, we won – the volleyball game and the food from the dogs.

PERFECT PICNIC: TOP TIPS

GET AHEAD

The majority of picnics take place at lunchtime. The light, the warmth, even sun we hope. Given that we not only have to pack up and to make our way there (and unpack), the more that can be done in advance, the better.

If it's a planned picnic (as opposed to a spontaneous last minute one) reading through recipes as far as possible in advance, to see whether there is anything that can be done the night beforehand, or even frozen, makes sense.

Try to spend a little time the evening before baking any goodies, making salad dressing, preparing crudités, packing the picnic basket and so forth. And remember to chill down any drinks, and to pop the freezer blocks in the freezer.

CHOOSING A MENU

Go through the motions of transporting the food before you decide on the menu (there must be an app for this). A plate of something to hand round might work if you are going to eat close to where you have parked, but if you have to negotiate a stile and lug it across several fields it will feel like an egg and spoon race. Again if you are using public transport this is going to be a no-no.

And then there is the time factor. A lovely roast whisked from your kitchen to the park and eaten slightly warm within a couple of hours, may not meet the demands of packing up a picnic in the morning when you are driving any distance to a play or opera and will be eating early evening.

THINK SMALL AND LIGHT

Picnics inevitably involve carrying, so the lighter, the better. I favour coldbags over boxes, and baskets over hampers, and try to keep any real crocks to a minimum, mixing them with some melamine or light ply. Try not to take more than you need of any one commodity; a chutney, mustard or other relish can be repackaged in Lilliputian-size jars, while salt and pepper can be scrunched up in a sachet of baking paper.

STAYING COOL

Cold water: Take a thermos flask of iced water, with plenty of ice-cubes in it. On a really hot day that sip of mountain cold water will be nirvana.

Wine and drinks: Err on the side of caution here and chill your drinks below the temperature you want to drink them at before leaving (an hour in the freezer should do it), which will allow for the opening and closing of the coldbag.

Ice packs: Remember to put these into the freezer the night before.

Chill sleeve: If you double up on the chilling by popping the wine into a cold sleeve and then inside a coldbag, you should cover yourself in a heatwave.

Ice: For a very hot day, fill a Thermos drinks or food flask with ice-cubes.

KEEPING WARM

Rugs: It is the easiest thing to underestimate how cold it can be (or become) after that swim in the sea on a picnic, when you are snug at home and the sun is shining through the kitchen window. I swear by lightweight fluffy fleece rugs that double as picnic rugs, ditto old-fashioned woollen car rugs.

Hot drinks: Picnics have a habit of taking on a sudden chill late afternoon, or when a cloud passes over and the breeze picks up, and there is nothing quite as civilised or restorative as a mug of warm hot chocolate, tea or coffee.

CHECK THE CHECKLIST

I don't need much of an excuse to make a list, but have a particular fondness for checklists and swear by consulting them as I am packing up. There is always something that I will have thought of at some point and then forgotten about.

PICNIC FAUX PAS

● Glasses with stems – why waste good wine?
● Old rugs with holes and stains – we're not pets. If you wouldn't use it indoors it won't do for outdoors. And you deserve a lovely new picnic rug.
● Too much melamine and plastic – soulless 'en masse', just a little in with the real crocks.
● Too many real crocks – too heavy, and fragile, but a few to provide a little glamour and risk.

● Vintage thermos flasks – these need to work, looking pretty is optional.
● Ugly plastic containers as serving dishes – the most special picnic can end up looking like a tupperware party unless we plan our servingware carefully. Better to wrap the food in foil, then transfer to a serving dish once there.
● Flimsy plastic cups – anywhere, ever, but paper ones curiously are fine.
● Swiss army knives – we're not hiking and they're too small to be of any real use slicing food.
● Plastic picnic tables – we'd rather sit on a rug even if it does challenge our joints. Or take a colourful cloth to disguise it.
● Campaign picnic chairs with integral drinks holders – we're not watching golf.
● DITTO over-sized stripey umbrellas – although if this is your biggest brolly.....
● An aerosol of fly-spray – so tempting.
● Wet wipes – nothing to wash the smell off afterwards. Better a thermos of water and a cloth.

PICNIC KIT

HAMPERS AND BASKETS

I like to put together my own hamper depending on what we are eating, those rather formal wicker baskets that come with cutlery strapped to the lid leave me feeling ill at ease. Most usually I opt for a big wicker basket and a stripey beach or other lightweight straw bag. This way we only take what we need. Sometimes the starting point is indeed a hamper, something that on occasions we get given filled with goodies, that are usefully employed thereafter. Wrap everything in linen napkins or tea-towels if it is likely to rattle around, and these can be used as cloths to spread the food on.

COLDBAGS

De rigeur, even if you take a hamper. I favour coldbags over boxes, which tend to be heavier and more bulky. The best come lined with insulating material, and you can hedge your bets with freezer blocks. Hard to have too many, a minimum of two if not three good-sized ones for an average picnic. Mini bags are also great for cans of drink.

CROCKS

The occasional real crocks can provide a civilising note, and if I am taking a plate of food or a tart, then I might transport it on a favourite vintage china plate. Most of my picnic kit consists of bits and bobs that I have amassed at car boot sales, or it may be the odds and ends of sets that have subsequently been broken or got lost. The result is a friendly mish-mash that works together as a whole because the last thing that matters on a picnic is matching plates and cutlery. It is then of little consequence if anything goes missing.

I also love wooden platters, the more distressed the better. There is a big revival in melamine, which is pretty much perfect for picnics as it is lightweight and unbreakable. But shop with care here as there is melamine and melamine, and the good stuff is something that wouldn't shame us at home. There is plenty of retro melamine on the market, that will cut a dash mingling with old crocks. Lightweight acrylic is also a good material, I particularly like clear tableware that could at a distance stand in for glass.

PLATES

If you go down the proper crock route it can get heavy, so this is where I tend to turn to paper or thin ply plates, not least because you can throw them away afterwards so there's no washing up involved. But otherwise, enamelware is ever brilliant, if you camp you're quids in as it's quite likely you have some of these in any case.

CUTLERY

For truly lightweight cutlery, wooden or ply is ideal. And the rather odd-sounding 'sporks' that combine spoon at one end with fork at the other, do make sense. There is some kitsch but pretty acetate picnic cutlery around too. On the real front, a selection of bone-handled odds and ends is more alluring than stainless steel. You can wrap these up in a napkin or clean tea-towel to transport, which will double as a small cloth once unwrapped.

GLASSES AND CUPS

I would forego all idea of glasses with stems, Champagne never tastes better than when drunk out of a tumbler, wine and cider ditto. My solution is a mish-mash of glasses that I collect in ones and twos from junk shops and sales. The other very useful type, are stainless steel shooting cups, which stack to nothing and are light. Or, serve your wine in small melamine or Bakelite mugs – baby's or children's ones come in just the right size.

CONTAINERS AND SERVING DISHES

Unless you are travelling a short distance from car to picnic, you will almost certainly want to pack food in an airtight container. The most efficient are Lock & Lock, that are air and liquid tight once you have clipped the wings into place (it is sod's law that many of the prettier coloured plastic ones are also least efficient). But you can always juggle here, and use the pretty sort for baked goods, stacking finger foods between layers of baking paper. And then transport anything likely to spill in a lockable container. Maybe take some lightweight acetate, melamine or bamboo bowls with you to transfer the food once you arrive, enamelled tin trays make excellent large serving plates too. Stackable sets of plastic containers have the advantage that once empty you can slot them within each other, and then pop them in a plastic bag to transport home. Cork is another favourite material, feather light and rustic. And look out for tiffin carriers, a brilliant system of stacking several different dishes on top of each other, and clamping the stack shut. These come with a carry handle.

The alternative for rustic chic are jam jars, good for sauces and relishes, a drop of milk or whatever. These could be Le Parfait clip-top jars which come in various sizes, or ones that you have collected over the years. Be sure to hang onto little jam jars, that might not make sense in terms of homemade preserves, but are ideal for any sauces, condiments or chopped herbs you want to take. And old-fashioned tins are good for baked treats.

THERMOS

It's worth taking a thermos of chilled water, if not for drinks, it'll come in handy for wiping down sticky fingers. Fill with water and lots of ice-cubes.

MINISCULE CHOPPING BOARD

The smallest possible chopping board serves for slicing salamis, cheeses and tomatoes, or cutting the base off a lettuce or head of chicory. The lighter the better, cork or bamboo are ideal.

TRAVELLING BARBECUE

Weber's 'Smokey Joe Gold', a miniature kettle barbecue with a lid, is a little bulkier than other portable types, but if you have the space it's a guarantee of great results. The handle clips over the lid so you can carry it without any ash falling out, or even move it around once it's lit. Most importantly, avoid disposable ones, but not without taking a leaf out of their book by loading your barbecue with briquettes and firelighters before you go.

RUBBISH BAGS

So important, for all those scraps at the end, and the dirty crocks. Take at least one large one, and then some small ones too, double–lined unless they are trusted not to leak on the way home.

FOOD BAGS AND TIES

A roll of these also comes in handy for transporting any leftovers back home.

CORKSCREW

If you are transporting the bottles upright, why not open them before you go? Some folding knives also usefully come with one attached, so you can keep it ready in the picnic bag.

SEA SALT AND BLACK PEPPER

Tastes differ, and it's as well to take a little seasoning for those that feel they want more. One route is to take a small sachet of the two mixed together, or a pill box. There are also some good travel and picnic designs around.

Knife Hall of Fame

FOLDING KNIVES

The most sophisticated outward-bound folding knives tend to come with a host of attachments that are redundant on a picnic, a corkscrew and bottle opener aside. The most useful folding knives are also some of the most elegant, a single blade is all we are after, but a slightly longer one than normal, some 12cm, that will serve us proud for slicing and cutting.

Opinel: Hard to imagine life without these iconic wooden and steel folding knives, so simple, reliable and beautifully designed. Still made entirely in France, by the descendants of Jospeh Opinel who designed the original in 1890. It comes in sizes ranging 1–12.

A rustic wooden-handled folding knife with a steel blade, the safety ring that locks the blade both open or closed was added at a later date. They are one of the cheapest solutions around, my choice is to give one to every diner when knives and forks are called for, as well as relying on them for slicing cheese, cake and the like.

Laguiole: I have a complete passion for these exquisite handmade folding knives, they are something to treasure for a lifetime, and I often give them as Christening or milestone presents. But beware of fakes, these must be one of the most copied articles outside of Gucci bags, as sadly the original artisanal producers failed to patent their design in time. Today there are just a handful of traditional forges making the knives.

The humble beginnings of the Laguiole knife go back to the early nineteenth century, to the village of the same name, home to an array of isolated farms. In the winter months, the family elders would migrate to Catalonia to work as sawyers, returning with a Spanish 'navaja' knife. The slender handle and yatagan-shaped blade of today's Laguiole took inspiration from these knives, which provided a blueprint.

There are any number of fascinating stories surrounding Laguiole knives that can be found on www.layole.com, the house of 'Honoré Durand', one of the best and very few artisanal forges. It is only recently that the tradition for artisanal production has once again established itself locally, having been eclipsed for decades by the mechanised industrial production at Thiers. The real thing involves some 109 different stages of craftsmanship, and the knife will come with a certificate of authenticity. A bee on the handle and the word Laguiole on the blade is not enough!

LamsonSharp Batard: This Desperate Dan-sized folding picnic knife (with corkscrew) was designed by Charles van Over, author of *The Best Bread Ever*, who insists that bread should be cut properly. But finding a serrated bread knife to take on a picnic all but impossible, he persuaded Lamson and Goodnow, the American manufacturers to team up and produced this. Its use goes far beyond bread.

KNIVES WITH GUARDS

Wusthof Trident: If you don't want to invest in special picnicware, my favourite range of kitchen knives by Wusthof Trident also come with knife guards. The Classic 16cm serrated sausage knife has long been my desert island choice, just big enough for slicing a loaf of bread, it makes short work of tomatoes, salamis or a roast.

Kuhn Rikon: These razor-sharp pop-coloured knives with protective shields deserve to become a modern classic. Designed for the Swiss manufacturer Kuhn Rikon by Philipp Beyeler, they come in a picnic-perfect range of bright jelly hues, with or without polka dots, gingham and the like. Their Japanese carbon steel blades defy the innocence of their appearance. And they're affordable.

Lounging

RUGS
For any more than two people, a couple of picnic rugs (or more) make sense and allow for spreading the picnic out and lazing full length at the same time. If the weather is dry then a plastic back doesn't really matter, although a heavy dew can leave the ground feeling damp for the best part of the day, so it's good to have at least one waterproof option up your sleeve. Thick woollen rugs are still a personal favourite, and these can also be found with plastic backs. Lightweight rugs that fold down to nothing, are again extremely useful.

CLOTHS
If you only have one rug, then use this for sitting on and spread out a cloth for the food. Lovely new linen tea-towels make great picnic cloths, anything jazzy that seems far too good to dry up with. Old-fashioned tray cloths are also a good size. Another option if the weather is dry is a thick linen-effect disposable cloth.

FLEECES
I like to take a warm fleece rug, for that extra comfort, many is the time it has doubled as a blanket as the chill sets in.

CUSHIONS
Nothing special here, just something small and light that you won't mind getting dirty, and/or wet.

PICNIC TABLES AND CHAIRS
There is a wonderful display in the Musée de la Chasse et de la Nature in Paris of a hunting picnic, with a low coffee-table-height table and cushions around it, by which all others will be judged. But, finding such a table is most likely to involve cutting down an inexpensive folding table to the required height.

Fishing stools make the simplest of chairs to perch on. Trawl eBay and you might even find them with a table, a neat arrangement where they slot inside the base of the table.

PICNIC LIGHTS
Solar outdoor lights have revolutionised the dusk or evening picnic. Folding Chinese lanterns and strings of lights are perfect for hanging in trees. Otherwise some tea-lights in small jars will cast the right kind of magic, as well as being protected from the wind.

WASP DETERRENT
For the wasp-phobe, of which I am one, it doesn't take more than a couple of the determined little creatures to send you back indoors. There is no rationale behind the hatred of these insects, but were a wasp to position itself between me and a pile of priceless china in a shop, I could do more damage than a bull. So a couple of 'waspinators' is a brilliant defence for the picknicker. These ingenious devices mimic a wasp nest, deterring the insects, which are terratorial by nature, making them think they are likely to be attacked if they go any closer. Lightweight and transportable, just hang a couple within the vicinity of the picnic and hope the wasps are sufficiently gullible.

'Tea-lights in small jars will cast the right kind of magic, as well as being protected from the wind.'

A CHECKLIST FOR PICNIC PERFECTION

I have a checklist pinned inside a cupboard door for what to pack on holiday that still reads 'baby bottles', 'drinking cup' and 'changing mat', even though my youngest son is now a teenager. But it also has things like 'passport', 'mobile', 'euros', 'house key' and I have to say it does the trick.

You may not need everything on the lists below, but run through it before leaving; it just might save you having to drive back home to get the picnic bag or corkscrew. We've all done that.

The Picnic list

The picnic food itself
Glasses
Mugs
Plates – eating and serving
Knives, forks, spoons
Folding knife
Corkscrew
Salt and pepper
Napkins
Small bread board
Tea-towels
Tablecloth clips
Food cover
Waspinator
Vacuum flask
Cold drinks
Hot drinks

If barbecuing:
Barbecue preloaded with briquettes and firelighters
Matches
Tongs
Sturdy plate or tray for the hot food

Paraphernalia
Sun hats
Suncream
Sunglasses
Umbrella
Waterproof
Picnic rugs
Fleece
Cushions
Stools or chairs
Picnic table
Kitchen roll
Clingfilm
Big and small plastic bags for leftovers
Games

RECIPE SYMBOLS GUIDE

These symbols appear next to the following recipes as a guide to enable you to easily match recipes to your picnic.

COMMUNAL
good to hand round when there are lots of people

GLAMOROUS
special occasion picnics

IN ADVANCE
can be made in advance of the day of the picnic

E ADDRESS BOOK

eBay for vintage picnic kit.

www.lakeland.co.uk for the best lightweight coldbags (their own brand), lined with flectalon, which works like a thermos. This reflective silvered material was originally developed for NASA astronauts in space. The food remains at the same temperature as when it is put into the bag, even when left in the sun. Two or three of these, which will pack inside each other when not in use, revolutionise outdoor eating. Lakeland also offer a great range of picnic kit in season, including lovely paper plates and napkins, acrylicware and practical solutions such as food covers.

www.emmabridgewater.co.uk for sturdy, beautifully made and designed melamine. As well as her plates, the baby mugs make quirky wine glasses. Her enamelled tins are also excellent, and her trays double as unbreakable serving dishes, great for handing a big plate of anything around.

www.layole.com One of the last remaining authentic forges making Laguiole knives. Have these customised to order with the handle, blade length and attachments of your choice, and your initials. Slicing a salami or hunk of cheese doesn't get more luxurious.

www.roullierwhite.com This elegant online living emporium tempts on any number of fronts, but seek out the Batard folding picnic knife.

www.inthehaus.co.uk for classic Wusthof knives with guards.

www.kuhnrikon.co.uk for razor-sharp colourful plastic picnic knives with protective guards.

www.notonthehighstreet.com This marketplace of small quirky companies makes a brilliant hunting ground for picnic rugs, bags, plastic containers and other useful outdoor accoutrement.

www.josephjoseph.com If the talented brothers who run this kitchen design business can't solve the problem, no-one can. Their designs are modern classics, and we want a whole range on our picnics – their grip tray, their salad servers, salad bowl with a carry-handle built into the rim, their two-in-one salt and pepper grinder, the list goes on and on.

www.greentulip.co.uk for eco-friendly 'Bambu' veneer picnicware and lightweight lacquered bamboo bowls in jazzy colours.

www.marksandspencer.com This household name is as good at picnicware as it is at the clothing essentials for which we rely on it. Sturdy acrylic, and inexpensive rugs and picnic bags.

www.surplusandoutdoor.com for classic enamelware, which will double as camping gear.

www.johnlewis.co.uk and **www.jwpltd.co.uk** for our favourite stackable sets of Lock & Lock containers, which are the original and still the best of their kind.

www.weber.com for the bijoux travelling 'Smokey Joe' barbecues in this season's colours.

www.amazon.co.uk for Thermos Work Series steel flasks which will keep food hot or cold for 24 hours, and Thermos multi-purpose food and drink flasks that come with an option of pourers – good for soup, porridge and the like.

www.waspinator.co.uk for a wasp and

environment-friendly solution to these hungry little pests. A couple of these mock nests fold up to nothing, hang them nearby and hope the resident wasps are fooled.

www.ikea.com will have a great range of inexpensive and well-designed picnic gear during any summer. We especially love their solar lanterns.

www.marimekko.fi for gorgeous bright textiles that are perfect on picnics. I love their big tea-towels, as well as their tablecloths. They also have great canvas carry-alls.

www.anorakonline.co.uk for brilliant lightweight but waterproof picnic cloths, the equivalent of a folding umbrella. Pop one of these into your handbag along with a folding knife and go.

www.atlanticblankets.com for luxurious, thick, traditional woollen rugs and picnic blankets in up-to-the-minute designs.

www.tartanrugs.com for good-quality waterproof backed picnic rugs.

www.zoeppritz.com for the softest, warmest fleece blankets in fab jewel-like colours, seek out this long-established German manufacturer.

www.jaqueslondon.co.uk for the most beautiful outdoor games, be it boules in a wooden box, or the chic volleyball and rounders sets in their familiar dark green canvas cases. These come perfectly packaged and designed for the picknicker who likes to play.

DIPS, PÂTÉS & COLD CUTS

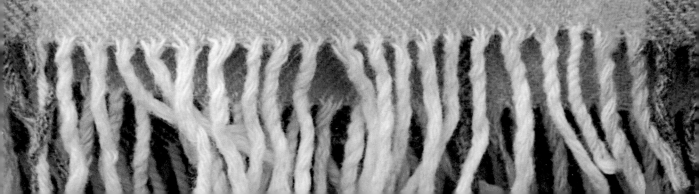

It is the prospect of feasting that

gets so many of us pulling out the hamper, the sheer plenty that goes hand in hand with the occasion. As a guest, trying to guess what lies within the cook's box of tricks makes for a tantalising game, as appetites are whetted by all that fresh air. The legendary exchange between Rat and Mole in Kenneth Grahame's *The Wind in the Willows* encapsulates it so perfectly, when in answer to Mole's wiggling curiosity of what is inside the wicker basket, Rat replies:
'There's cold chicken inside it…coldtonguecold-hamcoldbeefpickledgherkinssaladfrenchrolls-cresssandwichespottedmeatgingerbeerlemon-adesodawater'.

You don't have to unravel it (or be British) to get the point. It is almost worth lugging one of those heavy and wholly impractical hampers across a few fields for nothing more than the excitement of seeing a laden case, groaning with goodies set down on the grass and others wondering what could possibly lie within.

Well, for starters, cold meats, pâtés and little pots of deliciousness, we hope. Dipping and spreading are a large part of any relaxed picnic, a DIY bar for grazing with plentiful crudités, breads and pickles. There are lots of instant solutions: ready-made dips that can be jazzed up in a jiffy as a cheat's take on the real thing. In fact I felt slightly mortified recently on a picnic when my cheating dips seemed to attract more praise than anything else. But having repackaged them in attractive containers, I guess I asked for it.

For a slightly more soignée occasion, then a whole ham or some home-cured gravadlax (see page 45) are both readily accessible, can be made well in advance and will be streets ahead of anything that comes sliced and plastic-wrapped. One of the most enchanting picnics I have been on recently (or ever, in fact) was a dîner en blanc. I had never heard of these until I found myself in a communal garden dressed top to toe in white along with a couple of hundred other people dressed in a similar fashion, tables bedecked in white linen, with vases of white flowers and hundreds of white candles, lit as the sun was sinking (see page 39).

We shouldn't be too surprised to learn that dîner en blanc emanates from Paris, capital of chic, and they have actually been around for several decades. Just pop the search term dîner en blanc into Google images and you'll be met with a wonderful array of snaps, such as the one where some ten thousand picnickers took over the Place de la Concorde, all at fifteen minutes' notice of its whereabouts in order to foil any niggling authorities. It's the extreme in flash-mob dining, a massive Chinese whisper that starts doing the rounds courtesy of Twitter or a few well-placed texts to the right friends.

By comparison, we had plenty of warning for the one I attended – well, the luxury of twenty-four hours I seem to remember, though for a Londoner with a busy diary this still seemed on the racy side of spontaneous. And going back to where I started, the first course was so beautifully simple and right for the occasion: a large roast ham and equally large piece of Parmesan laid out on a trestle table with its own white linen cloth.

'It's worth lugging one of those heavy hampers across a few fields for the excitement of seeing a laden case, groaning with goodies.'

LET'S GO: DIPS

We love damning convenience foods, but where would most of us be without those plastic tubs of hummus, guacamole and the like. A lot of it isn't bad at all, but that small homemade touch injects an essential element of nurture. In pretty much every case there are invariably one or two finishes that will bring out the best in the dip. Or, you could go further, as it takes little longer to whizz up a creamy dip using soured cream or Greek yogurt. Rustle up some crudités and olives and you are well on your way to a respectable feast of a picnic.

HUMMUS

Stir ½ teaspoon of ground **cumin** into a 300g tub of **hummus**. Transfer this to a portable container or bowl, drizzle over a little **extra virgin olive oil** and a squeeze of **lemon juice** and dust with a little more cumin.
For 4–6 people

GUACAMOLE

Stir 2 teaspoons of finely chopped **coriander leaves** into a 200g tub of **guacamole**. Transfer this to a portable container or bowl, drizzle over a little **extra virgin olive oil**, dust with **cayenne pepper** and scatter over a little more coriander.
For 4 people

TARAMASALATA

Stir ½ teaspoon of finely grated **lemon zest** and a tablespoon of finely chopped **parsley** into a 200g tub of **taramasalata**. Transfer to a portable container or bowl, drizzle over a little **extra virgin olive oil** and a squeeze of **lemon juice** and scatter over some more parsley.
For 4 people

TZATZIKI

Stir 1 teaspoon of **extra virgin olive oil** and 2 teaspoons of finely chopped **mint** into a 200g tub of **tzatziki**. Transfer to a portable container or a bowl, drizzle over some more oil and scatter over a few tiny mint leaves.
For 4 people

CHEAT'S AIOLI

The short cut to making an aioli uses soured cream instead of mayonnaise. It makes for an elegant dip, as well as a sauce that can be slathered over food from the grill or cold roast beef (see page 115).

Blend 300g **soured cream**, 2 peeled and crushed **garlic cloves**, ½ tablespoon of **lemon juice** and a little **sea salt** in a bowl and spoon into a clean bowl or container. Chill until required. Before you leave the house, dust the top with **Piment d'Espelette or cayenne pepper**.
For 8–10 people

CREAMED GOAT'S CHEESE

This creamy dip can be tinkered with endlessly, using different ingredients and flavourings depending on what you want to serve it with, but roasted vegetables are always a good starting point, as is a bowl of feisty green leaves with a walnut dressing.

Whizz 250g **fresh young goat's cheese** with 100g **Greek yogurt or fromage blanc** and 100g **crème fraîche** in a food-processor until creamy. It will probably be slightly grainy, but that's fine. Transfer to a bowl and stir in 2 tablespoons of finely snipped **chives**. Chill until required. Before you leave for the picnic, dust with **paprika**.
For 6 people

LABNA

This light, herbed cream cheese is no more arduous to prepare than the preceding instantly drummed-up dips, except that this one needs to be left overnight. Delicious with bresaola, coppa, échine de porc séchée and other such delicate cured meats.

For 4–6 people

500g Greek yogurt
1 tablespoon each of finely chopped mint, chives and flat-leaf parsley
½ teaspoon sea salt
cayenne pepper or Piment d'Espelette, for dusting

Blend the yogurt with the herbs and salt. Tip this into a fine-mesh sieve (or one lined with a clean tea-towel) set over a large bowl and chill for 24 hours. Spoon what remains in the sieve or tea-towel into a bowl or container and smooth the surface. Dust with cayenne pepper or Piment d'Espelette before leaving.

Kit Serving spoon, plate, table knife

DUCK RILLETTES

Rillettes rely on meat that is cooked for so long that it gives up all resistance and falls into succulent shreds at the pressure of a fork. This is a cheat's take.

For 6–8 people

1 x 1-litre jar confit of duck or goose, at room temperature (contains 750g meat, approx. 400g shredded weight)
a pinch each of ground cinnamon, cloves, nutmeg and allspice
1 tablespoon thyme leaves
3 tablespoons Cointreau or Grand Marnier
sea salt and black pepper

Tip the confit into a medium saucepan and gently heat through for about 10 minutes, turning the meat halfway through. Transfer it to a plate and take it off the bone, discarding any fat. Shred it using two forks and transfer it to a large bowl. Add the spices and thyme.

Strain the fat and juices into a bowl and measure out 200ml of fat. Assuming the confit had a pool of jellied juices in the bottom, pour these into a small saucepan, add the liqueur and simmer to reduce to a couple of tablespoons of sticky glaze. Mix these into the shredded meat, then add the reserved 200ml of fat and season to taste.

Pack the mixture into a ½ litre Le Parfait jar, pressing the mixture down well to exclude any air bubbles. Cover and chill. It should keep well for a couple of weeks.

Kit Plate, table knife

POTTED HAM WITH CORNICHONS

This is one step on from sliced roast ham, that not only passes the travel test with flying colours but conveniently comes with the butter and relish all in. Something in the way of crudités, such as celery hearts, and a hearty chunk of bread and you are done. You can pack it into a big dish for communal appreciation, or into individual pots or ramekins for a more glamorous affair.

For 6 people

200–300g unsalted butter
1 heaped teaspoon wholegrain mustard
400g roast ham, fat removed and diced
50g baby cornichons, sliced
4 tablespoons coarsely chopped flat-leaf parsley, plus extra leaves to decorate

Heat 100g of the butter in a large frying pan over a lowish heat and stir in the mustard. Add the ham, then fold in the cornichons and parsley.

Pack the mixture either into six 150ml ramekins or into a larger dish or two, pressing it down well, and wipe the rims with kitchen paper. Cover with clingfilm and chill for an hour or two until the butter sets.

Decorate the ramekins or dishes with parsley leaves, then melt the remaining butter in a small saucepan (the amount you will need here will depend on the surface area to be sealed; shallow dishes will call for more than deep ones), skim off the surface foam, pour the clear butter over the top (discarding the milky residue at the bottom), pressing the leaves down to submerge them. Chill for another hour or two until set and then cover.

Kit Serving spoon, plate, table knife

FARMHOUSE CHICKEN LIVER PÂTÉ

This silky pâté is a staple in our house and it freezes well, so it's a good one for that getting-ready-in-advance picnic. Dish it up with some chutney, radishes, gherkins and pickled onions and some grainy brown bread, and all you need are a couple of cheeses in addition. It's unusual to come across fresh chicken livers, so look out for them in the frozen-foods section.

For 4–6 people

225g unsalted butter
225g chicken livers, fatty membranes removed
1 bay leaf
2 sprigs of thyme
sea salt and black pepper

1 shallot, peeled and finely chopped
1 garlic clove, peeled and finely chopped
2 tablespoons Calvados or brandy
1 tablespoon crème fraîche
freshly grated nutmeg

Melt 25g of the butter in a large frying pan over a medium heat. When the foam starts to subside add the chicken livers and the herbs, season and sauté for 3 minutes until the chicken livers are golden on the outside but still pink in the centre, turning them halfway through cooking. Discard the herbs and tip the livers with any juices into a blender.

Add another knob of butter to the pan and fry the shallot and garlic for a couple of minutes until glossy and translucent. Add the Calvados or brandy to the pan and simmer until it has all but disappeared. Tip the contents of the frying pan into the blender and purée with the crème fraîche.

Leave this to cool for about 20 minutes, then dice and add the remaining butter and blend until the pâté is really smooth and creamy. Add a grating of nutmeg and adjust the seasoning. (I like to pass the pâté through a fine sieve to ensure it's as silky as possible, but you don't have to.)

Spoon the pâté into a jar or a bowl, smooth the surface, cover and chill until required. It keeps well for at least 48 hours in the fridge.

Kit Plate, table knife

POTTED CRAB

Like shrimps, crab makes a delicious buttery pâté for piling on a crust of bread, with a few salad leaves or radishes in attendance. In fact, this picnic treat is one of the best uses for crab that I can think of, where the brown meat is as readily employed as the white. Just find a grassy dune or a hillock with a good view of the sea to enhance it.

For 6 people

150g unsalted butter
375g white and brown crabmeat, picked over
juice of ½ lemon
1/3 teaspoon ground mace
1/3 teaspoon cayenne pepper
sea salt
1 bay leaf

Melt 100g of the butter in a small frying pan over a medium heat, add the crabmeat and stir until heated through. Add the lemon juice, mace, cayenne pepper and a little salt to taste. Pack this into a bowl, cover and chill for about 1 hour until it firms. Melt the remaining butter in a small saucepan, lay a bay leaf over the surface of the crab and pour over the butter. Cover and chill. This will keep well for a couple of days in the fridge.

Kit Plate, table knife

POTTED SMOKED SALMON WITH LEMON

That little bit more luxurious than a pâté. Smoked salmon always welcomes a few drops of fresh lemon juice at the last minute. I've always loved those lemon halves wrapped in muslin that are the domain of seafood bars, but also a good ruse on a picnic, tied at the pointed end with thin string or white ribbon. Failing a rich curd cheese, you could use 180g full-fat fromage blanc seasoned with salt and pepper, and 20g of clotted or Jersey cream.

For 6 people

200g rich curd cheese
1 teaspoon finely grated lemon zest*
a generous pinch of ground mace
a couple of shakes of Tabasco
400g smoked salmon, brown meat cut out, diced
2 tablespoons small capers, rinsed and patted dry
2 tablespoons finely chopped chives

Blend the curd cheese, lemon zest, mace and Tabasco in a large bowl and fold in the smoked salmon. Pack into six little pots or a larger bowl, and wipe the rims with kitchen paper. Scatter over the capers and chives, although save doing this until the morning of the picnic if making these more than a day in advance, and chill. They should keep for several days in the fridge.

Kit Plate, table knife

*****Tip** Use a grater not a zester here.

MACKEREL RILLETTES

Mackerel is a deliciously succulent and moist fish, and combining fresh with the smoked version gives you the best of both worlds. Here, rillettes make a virtuously healthy pâté, with lots of fish oils boosted by some extra virgin olive oil. I'd dish this up with some crisp croûtons (see page 53), and perhaps some radishes and gherkins.

For 6 people

300–400g fresh mackerel fillets (approx.
   600–700g of whole fish)
300g smoked mackerel fillets
2 bay leaves
3 garlic cloves, peeled and halved lengthways
black pepper
100ml white wine
50ml water
a squeeze of lemon juice
3 tablespoons extra virgin olive oil
2 spring onions, trimmed and finely sliced
sea salt

Arrange the fresh and smoked mackerel fillets over the base of a large saucepan. Add the bay leaves and garlic and grind over some black pepper. Pour over the wine and 50ml water, bring to the boil, cover and cook for 2 minutes over a medium heat, then remove from the heat and leave to cool for several hours.

Pour the liquid into a small saucepan and simmer to reduce to a couple of tablespoons of liquid in total. Flake the fish into a bowl, discarding any bones and skin, including the tough surface skin on the smoked fillets. Pour over the reduced liquor, a squeeze of lemon juice and 2 tablespoons of olive oil, and gently mix in two thirds of the spring onion, trying not to break up the flakes. Taste and add a little salt if you think it needs it.

Tip the rillettes into a clean bowl or jar with an airtight lid and chill. Drizzle over another tablespoon of oil and scatter over the remaining spring onion before setting off for your picnic.

Kit Serving spoon, plate, table knife

MAPLE ROAST HAM

Roast hams make as much of a star turn at a picnic as they do on the Christmas table, be it at that dîner en blanc (see page 39), or any other occasion when you are trying to cater for eight or ten friends and want something wholly practical but rather special too.

Should you be any more in number, then you could roast a couple of chickens or buy a round of Brie or another gooey cheese. It is worth checking with your butcher when buying the ham whether or not it needs soaking overnight. Mostly a change of water in the process of cooking will do the trick.

For 6–8 people

1 x 2kg unsmoked gammon, boned
  and rolled
3 outer stalks of celery, trimmed and sliced
2 carrots, trimmed and sliced
1 leek, trimmed and sliced
2 bay leaves
2 tablespoons maple syrup
1 teaspoon treacle
2 teaspoons English mustard

Place the gammon in a large saucepan (I use a preserving pan), cover with cold water and bring to the boil. Discard the water and start again with fresh water to cover, this time adding the chopped vegetables and bay leaves. Bring to the boil, then maintain at a gentle simmer over a low heat for 50 minutes. If necessary, top up with boiling water halfway through.

Heat the oven to 180°C fan/190°C/gas mark 6. Transfer the ham from the saucepan onto a board using two forks (the stock makes excellent soup, although it may need reducing). Remove any string around the ham and pull off the rind. Slice the fat at 2cm intervals with a criss-cross pattern, without cutting down as far as the flesh.

Blend the maple syrup, treacle and mustard in a bowl and use this to coat the ham evenly all over. If you like you can also tie another couple of pieces of string around the joint if it seems loose. Place the ham in a roasting tin and pour a few millimetres of the ham stock into the base to prevent any syrup that trickles down from burning. Roast for 35–45 minutes until the glaze is mahogany-coloured and dry. Leave the ham to cool. If you carve it at home before setting off wrap it up tightly in foil to transport.

Kit Plate, serving fork

GRAVADLAX

Passionate as I am about cooking I tend to draw the line at home-smoking and making bread. Gravadlax, however, is the easiest cured fish to prepare and enormously satisfying to make. And, most importantly, you can guarantee the quality of your salmon in the first place, something that gets harder and harder when you buy cured salmon ready-prepared and sliced. The ideal section is from the thickest part of a whole fish – ask for it to be filleted into two pieces, leaving the skin on, but don't fret if it turns out differently. This is a good dish to freeze, even ready sliced, and makes an elegant centrepiece. Lovely laid on a slice of buttered soda or rye bread, but equally delicious on a small crisp lettuce leaf.

For 6–8 people

100g rock salt
100g caster sugar
20g yellow mustard seeds
a small bunch of dill or chervil (approx. 20g),
   finely chopped, plus 2 tablespoons to serve
900g salmon fillet, skin-on, pin bones removed
Little Gem heart leaves or buttered soda or rye
   bread, to serve

MUSTARD SAUCE

Blend 150g **soured cream**,1 rounded tablespoon **Dijon mustard**,1 rounded tablespoon **wholegrain mustard**,1 scant tablespoon **caster sugar** together in a bowl. Leave to stand for 10 minutes to allow the sugar to dissolve, then stir again. Chill until required.

Combine the salt, sugar, mustard seeds and dill (or chervil) in a bowl. Scatter a quarter of the salt mixture over a piece of clingfilm large enough to wrap the two fillets up in when placed on top of each other. Place one fillet skin-down on top, scatter over two thirds of the remaining mixture, then lay the second fillet on top so the thick part of the fillet is on top of the thin part of the fillet, and they lie flesh to flesh. Scatter over the remaining salt mixture, wrap the salmon up, and then in foil.

Two heavy cast iron roasting dishes that fit inside each other provide the best route to curing and weighting the fish. Place the salmon inside the larger dish and place the smaller dish on top (anything lighter will require weighting with a tin can or two). Chill for 48 hours, turning the parcel every 12 hours. During this time the sugar and salt will draw the juices out of the salmon and turn into a sticky brine.

Unwrap the salmon and rinse the marinade off the flesh-side. Some of the mustard seeds and dill should remain but you will get rid of the excess salt and sugar. Place the fillets skin-down on the work surface, then place a kitchen paper over each fillet and press to absorb any excess liquid, and repeat. Press the 2 tablespoons of finely chopped dill into the surface.

Trim the edge of the fillets if very thin, then slice the gravadlax diagonally off the skin, thicker than you would smoked salmon, discarding the ends. Serve with some mustard sauce.

Kit Spoon, plate

BREADS, TARTS & PIES

We seem to spend a great deal of

our time planning for the future instead of living in the present. And perhaps this is one reason why so often spontaneous last-minute picnics prove the most magical. They come as a lovely surprise that you haven't factored into your jam-packed diary, until you happen to wake up to a crystal-clear blue sky on a weekend morning and think, why not, let's go.

One reason why not, I suppose, is children, and if I am honest I think I did more of this before having a family, but I still cling to the idyll. Especially when I think back to one rather perfect lunch when we took off to a water-meadow just outside Henley and parked ourselves along with a posse of friends on a thin strip of land hemmed in by a field of rape in full flower on one side and by the River Thames on the other, with the enchanting folly Temple Island in the middle. To this day I can recall the luminous yellow of the oilseed rape (I have looked fondly on this crop ever since) set against the bottomless blue of the sky, there was an alluring faint chill in the air befitting the entrance to the

Chiltern Hills visible in the distance.

The starting point for almost any such opportunism is good bread. Now as one of life's freezer-phobes, bread is an exception and one of the few items that I do keep frozen. Good bread is hard to find so I buy a loaf or two whenever I happen to chance across it. It defrosts in no time, you don't even need to plan as far as the night before, a couple of hours at an ambient temperature and it should be deliciously soft and fresh.

And then, of course, you want lots of lovely bits and pieces to adorn its crumb. You may well have some of the essentials – I'm thinking olives and soft semi sun-dried tomatoes, maybe some onions in balsamic vinegar, pickled chillies and a jar of artichokes in oil – that you can call on. Then again you may not, in which case it's a quick trip to the shops. So, all that is left is the need for cheese and cold cuts and, again, given these are keepers you may be able to pad out with what you have to hand. Tinned sardines in chilli oil are a staple of my storecupboard, gorgeous with a crust of bread and ripe tomatoes. It could be that simple.

'Good bread is hard to find so I buy a loaf or two whenever I happen to chance across it.'

LET'S GO: DIY SANDWICH BAR

What follows is really a reminder of the sort of goodies that are ripe for assembling a DIY sandwich bar once you get there. The only possible guideline is perhaps to think of grouping ingredients with the same geographical leanings together: for instance, fill focaccia with tapenade, goat's cheese, artichokes in oil, roasted peppers and rocket; or pile salt beef, gherkins and sauerkraut onto buttered rye; marry Black Forest ham with smoked cheese. However you play it, the idea is zero preparation, just pack and go.

BREADS

Baguettes, sourdough loaves, rye bread, focaccia and petit pains, crusty wholegrain loaves, bridge rolls and carta di musica.

SPREADS

Tapenade, hummus (see page 30), taramasalata (see page 30), sun-dried tomato paste, pesto, cream cheese and mayonnaise.

SUNDRIES

Sun-dried tomatoes in oil, pitted green and black olives, artichokes in oil, grilled peppers in oil, caper berries, pickled chillies, grilled courgettes, salted anchovies, crab, smoked cod's roe, peeled prawns, cocktail gherkins and sauerkraut.

CHUTNEYS

Cranberry sauce, apricot chutney and sweet tomato and chilli relish (see page 58).

SALAD

Rocket, watercress, mustard and cress, flat-leaf parsley, baby leaves, salad sprouts, basil, cucumber, radishes and cherry tomatoes.

COLD CUTS

Air-dried ham, roast ham, salami, mortadella, salt beef and pastrami.

CHEESES

Feta, Parmesan slivers, buffalo mozzarella, Roquefort, Fourme d'Ambert, Gouda, Cantal, Gruyère, Brie, Gorgonzola, Manchego, Cheddar and Lancashire.

PICNIC REUBENS

This classic German sandwich, championed by New Yorkers, is usually served hot, but makes a great picnic dish too. Pile **buttered rye bread** with fine slivers of **Gruyère or Comté**, **sauerkraut**, **pastrami** and **Russian dressing** (3 heaped tablespoons **mayonnaise**, 1 heaped tablespoon **tomato ketchup**, 1 heaped teaspoon **horseradish sauce**, ½ teaspoon **Worcestershire sauce**).

PROPER CROÛTONS

It is one thing to plunder the dank interior of a good cheese shop, and ask the butcher to set his slicer on its finest setting for that haunch of air-dried ham on display. But good croûtons? Even the very French neighbourhood patisserie is likely to fail on this one, and there is nothing quite like them for scooping up a gooey Gorgonzola or Brie de Meaux, or a spoon of silky chicken liver pâté (see page 37). Deliciously crisp and delicate, you want a refined baguette here rather than a 'baguette de tradition' or sourdough type. These can be rustled up a day or two in advance of a picnic.

Preheat the oven to 180°C fan/190°C/gas mark 6. Slice a slim **baguette** about 0.5cm thick for slim croûtons, or 1cm thick for more robust ones. Lay them out on baking sheets and toast in the oven for 5 minutes until they have dried out. Paint each side with **olive oil** and return to the oven for another 5–8 minutes, depending on their thickness, or until they are golden-brown and crisp. Leave them to cool before transferring to a plastic food bag or container.

CRUSTY GARLIC OLIVE BREAD

This picnic loaf has garlic-bread-like charm, soaked in olive oil infused with garlic, with olives and also herbs for good measure.

Makes ½ baguette or 1 small baton

Blend 4 tablespoons **extra virgin olive oil** together with 1 crushed **garlic clove**, 2 tablespoons finely chopped **green or black olives** and 1 tablespoon of **lemon thyme leaves**. Halve a **small baton or half a baguette** lengthways, leaving the halves attached at the side and open it out. Drizzle the mixture over the two cut surfaces, spreading the olives out evenly, then wrap it up in foil.

Bake for 15 minutes at 180°C fan/190°C/gas mark 6, turning it over halfway through if you remember. Leave it wrapped in foil for easy transporting – it will still be delicious at an ambient temperature.

BREAD AND TOMATOES

I have an enduring love of tomatoes with bread in pretty much every form, from an Italian soup to the English breakfast treat of warm soft, grilled tomatoes mashed into a slice of buttered toast.

Lovely ripe heirloom varieties are one of summer's gifts, pack up a few carefully chosen specimens and a hearty loaf of bread, with an elegant Sicilian or Provencal extra virgin olive oil and a coarse sea salt, and you have one of life's great rustic picnics. Take it one step further and you can whizz up a tray of Majorcan 'pa amb oli' or bruschettas, for handing round.

PA AMB OLI

Like bruschettas in Italy, 'pa amb oli' is symbolic of Majorcan food. This particular take on bread and tomatoes captures the spirit of this small island in the Mediterranean. Traditional Majorcan bread is neither white nor brown but somewhere in between, does not contain salt and uses natural leavening. In character it is close-grained and relatively dry, so a rye bread or a light wholemeal are ideal substitutes. I like to make this using the lower half of a slipper-shaped loaf of rye and cut it thickly Into fingers. It will lap up almost any amount of olive oil, so it's worth taking an extra small bottle to the picnic to give it a final dousing before handing them round.

For 4 people

Heat a ridged griddle over a high heat and toast the bottom half of a long loaf of **rye bread** or **light wholemeal**, (cut 2–3cm deep) either side, pressing down with a spatula until it brands with stripes – if necessary trim the ends so that it fits. Give the crumb-side a few half-hearted swipes with a peeled **garlic clove**, and coat with a slug or two of **extra virgin olive oil**. Your **tomatoes** (you will need a couple of large, juicy plum tomatoes or maybe three smaller ones) should be ripe to the point of bursting, if they haven't already done so use a knife to make an incision and break them open using your fingers, working over the toast. Squeeze the seeds over the crumb, then mash the flesh onto the surface and throw away the skin and core. Crumble over a few flakes of **sea salt** and splash over a little more oil. Cut diagonally into 3cm-wide strips and arrange on a plate. These will be good for at least a couple of hours. Splash over a little more oil before serving.

TOMATO AND ANCHOVY PAN BAGNAT

Another play on bread and tomatoes, this time super-sweet slowly roasted cocktail tomatoes fill a hollowed-out loaf of bread, along with some anchovy fillets and rocket.

For 4–6 people

1 x 400g sourdough loaf or a small cottage loaf
3 tablespoons extra virgin olive oil
300g slow-roast tomatoes (see page 95)
30g rocket
10 salted anchovy fillets

Cut off the top third of the loaf to create a lid, and pull out the inside crumb from both the base and the lid, to leave a shell about 1cm thick. The insides can be whizzed in a food-processor to use as breadcrumbs and popped into the freezer.

Drizzle the oil over the cut surfaces, including the rim of both halves, spreading it evenly with a spoon. Spoon two thirds of the tomatoes into the base, lay half the rocket on top, then the anchovies, and then the remaining rocket. Spoon the remaining tomatoes into the lid, then carefully replace this. Wrap the loaf up snugly in clingfilm, place in a baking dish and place another lightweight dish on top with either a can or a jar – you want the loaf to be firm enough to slice without actually squashing it. Chill for a couple of hours.

Kit Serrated knife, plate

BRUSCHETTA

I remember driving through the Tuscan hills on our way to Montepulciano in Italy, when we chanced upon a hilltop café that had a large tray of bruschettas on the counter (in any other country I suspect this would have been classified as stale bread and tomatoes), but bought and consumed in the corner of a Tuscan field, invisibly laced with genius loci, I have been striving to recapture the magic of those tomatoes on toast ever since. In its basic incarnation bruschetta is a soggy affair of over-ripe tomatoes and lots of very green olive oil (green both in colour and in flavour), absorbed by a sturdy slice of toasted white bread. A French 'pain de campagne' is probably the most widely available crumb that suits, or a sourdough, but I'd avoid the poor over-exposed ciabatta.

For 4 people

Toast four thick slices of **coarsely textured white bread** and, depending on whether it feels sufficiently summery, give it a few half-hearted swipes with a peeled **garlic clove** – be very pathetic about this, a hint of garlic is fine but nothing too boisterous. Place the toast on a plate and coat with a slug or two of **extra virgin olive oil**. Your **tomatoes** (about four) should be ripe to the point of bursting at the seams, if they haven't already done so use a knife to make an incision and break them open with your fingers, working over the toast. Squeeze out the seeds, these are one of best bits of the tomato that fashion would have us discard, then mash the flesh onto the surface and throw away the skin and core. Crumble over a few flakes of **sea salt**. These will be good for at least a couple of hours. Splash over a little more oil before serving.

BREAD AND CHEESE

There's hardly a nation that doesn't have a contribution to make here, skirting the dairy-free zones of Asia, we can pretty much travel the world on a buttered roll filled with cheese and know exactly where we are on the map. It might be a doorstep of granary eaten with a mature farmhouse Cheddar, tomato chutney and pickled onions (the Great British tradition of Ploughman's), or Jarlsberg with a wholegrain 'grovbrød' if we travel north to Norway, or, if we happen to be lucky enough to be lazing in the shade of an olive grove in Tuscany, some of that long-lasting unsalted 'filone' with a hunk of ewe's milk 'Pecorino Toscano'.

Wearing my practical hat, then, I should advise you to stick to hard cheeses: a mature **Gouda**, **Cheddar** or **Cantal** (its French counterpart); and **hard sheep's or goat's cheeses,** such as **Spanish Manchego**, but this is to forego the delight of living dangerously and unwrapping a badly behaved **Époisses**, a cheese that is probably best eaten outdoors. You can always bury the remains rather than lugging them back home again.

Pan out your finds with a relish, some unshelled nuts and big bunches of grapes, and some figs or whatever other fruit is in season. Any hearty bread is good, a sourdough or a wholegrain, but there is no real need for butter, a bunch of watercress, perhaps, or some other that pays lipservice to green and leafy.

OVEN-BAKED SWEET TOMATO AND CHILLI RELISH

Challenged to a competition to come up with the most ways of consuming a sweet tomato and chilli relish, my family would eat any other for breakfast. Pared down to the bare minimum, this take on it is cooked in the oven so there's no hovering over the stove. It will last in the fridge for many weeks, unless your surname is Bell.

Makes approx. 400–500ml (1–2 jam jars)

1kg vine tomatoes
¾ teaspoon sea salt
200g granulated jam sugar with pectin
1 tablespoon finely chopped medium-hot red chilli
3 garlic cloves, peeled and finely chopped
100ml white wine or cider vinegar.

Preheat the oven to 180°C fan/190°C/gas mark 6. Bring a large pan of water to the boil, cut out a cone from the top of each tomato to remove the core and plunge them into the boiling water for about 20 seconds, and then into cold water. Slip off the skins and coarsely chop them. Combine all the ingredients in a large roasting dish (25 x 35cm) and place in the oven, uncovered, for 65–75 minutes, giving the relish a stir towards the end. It should reduce considerably, with the tomatoes sitting in a small amount of syrupy juices. Spoon it into a hot sterilised jar, or jars, cover and leave to cool. Store in the fridge.

EGG MAYONNAISE SALADINIS

Those on carb-free regimes can find picnics quite challenging, the role played by bread and tarts being the starring one that it is. So, these 'saladinis' are a great stand-in, but if carbs aren't an issue then buttered buns with egg mayonnaise are ever a joy.

On record we may have foresworn sliced white for wholegrain, but this doesn't include retro bridge rolls, that soft cushion with its fey flimsy crust. The shape of bridge rolls makes these a winner for handing round at picnics, and you could of course make them up as closed rolls and cut them in half, in which case you will need twice as many, but they are rather dainty in their open form.

Anchovies are particularly savoury and fine here, but egg mayonnaise can be partnered with all manner of goodies – a thick wodge of mustard and cress, air-dried ham or crispy snippets of bacon, sun-dried tomatoes or a teaspoon of salmon or trout roe if you want to up the ante. Or, if asked to bring a plate of something to a celebratory picnic, make up two or three of these, as well as some 'saladinis'.

Makes 6–8

5 medium eggs
4 tablespoons mayonnaise
sea salt and black pepper

approx. 3 Little Gem hearts, outer leaves
    discarded, or 3–4 finger or bridge rolls
6–8 anchovy fillets, halved lengthways
unsalted butter, softened for spreading (optional)

Bring a medium pan of water to the boil, lower in the eggs using a spoon and boil for 10 minutes. Drain and refill the pan with cold water and leave the eggs to cool. Now shell them and cut off and discard the top centimetre or so of white. Mash the yolks with the mayonnaise and a little seasoning to a coarse paste, in a bowl, and finely chop and fold in the whites. You can make the egg mayonnaise up to 24 hours in advance, in which case cover and chill it.

For saladinis
Separate out the Little Gem hearts. You want leaves some 7cm long, and reserve anything bigger or smaller for a salad. Fill with the egg mayonnaise and drape a strip of anchovy on top of each one.

For rolls
Slice a thin sliver off the top of the bridge rolls and slit in half (you can also slice the base crust off if desired). Butter (if wished) and spread with the egg mayonnaise and drape a couple of anchovy strips on top of each one.

RETRO CLUBS

Little squared sarnies are great when you want to make a big plate of something.

Makes approx. 25

approx. 8 slices honey-roast ham,
 fat removed
Dijon mustard
unsalted butter, softened for spreading
8 slices of white bread (medium), crusts
 removed
½ cucumber, peeled and thinly sliced
approx. ⅔ x 200g jar pimento-stuffed
 green olives

Line a 23cm square tin (ie brownie tin) with clingfilm, with enough overhanging the sides to fold back over the top. Arrange half the ham in a layer over the base and spread with a little mustard. Lightly butter the bread on either side and arrange a layer on top of the ham, cutting it to fit the tin. Lay the cucumber in a single layer on top in rows of overlapping slices, then top with more bread, spread with a little mustard and finish with the ham. Fold the overhanging clingfilm over the top and press the sandwich down with your hands.

Open the clingfilm up, turn the sandwich onto a board and peel off the clingfilm that lined the base. Tidy the edges using a bread knife and then cut into about 25 little square sandwiches. Skewer each one with an olive, sticking the cocktail stick through the stack. Carefully remove to a serving plate using a palette knife. These can be made well in advance, the night before if wished, in which case chill and keep them covered in clingfilm to transport.

SMOKED SALMON AND CREAM CHEESE ROLLS

The best smoked salmon rolls and bagels come with a thick blanket of soft creamy cheese laced with chives, and peppered with cayenne. These are another good plate for sharing, either cut in half or in quarters. Mini-bagels are also an option, but ultimately any roll will do.

Makes 4

Cream cheese
150g cream cheese
50g fromage frais
a generous squeeze of lemon juice
a few drops of onion juice (squeezed
 through a garlic press)
2 tablespoons finely chopped chives
Rolls
unsalted butter, softened for spreading
 (optional)
4 rolls, slit
200g sliced smoked salmon
cayenne pepper
watercress sprigs, to serve (optional)

Blend the cream cheese and fromage frais in a bowl, then blend in the lemon and onion juice, and mix in the chives. Butter the rolls, if wished, and spread the cream cheese on the lower half, top with smoked salmon, dust with cayenne and arrange a few sprigs of watercress on top, if wished. Close and halve or quarter.

ANCHOVY BUNS

Smaller than a muffin, made in a fairy-cake tin, these are of a size that leaves plenty of space to sample everything else on offer. Lovely on their own, it's tempting to dish them up with soured cream and salmon roe too.

Makes 12

40g unsalted butter, melted, plus extra for
   greasing
150g plain flour
1 heaped teaspoon baking powder, sifted
sea salt
cayenne pepper
2 medium eggs
100ml milk
6 salted anchovy fillets, thinly sliced
6 spring onions, trimmed and thinly sliced
1 teaspoon extra virgin olive oil

Preheat the oven to 180°C fan/190°C/gas mark 6, and liberally grease a 12-bun fairy cake tin with butter. Combine the flour, baking powder, a pinch of salt and of cayenne pepper in a large bowl. Whisk the eggs and milk in another large bowl, then stir in the melted butter. Pour this mixture onto the dry ingredients and blend to a lumpy batter. Fold in the anchovies and three quarters of the spring onions and half fill the moulds with the mixture.

Toss the reserved spring onion with the olive oil and scatter this over the top of the buns. Bake for 15–17 minutes until golden and crusty. These can also be rewarmed for 5–10 minutes in an oven heated to 170°C fan/180°C/gas mark 5 to refresh them if they are a day or two old.

CHEESE AND ONION MUFFINS

A classic combination that never fails.

Makes 12

225g plain flour
75g fine cornmeal
50g finely grated pecorino
1 tablespoon baking powder
½ teaspoon sea salt
3 medium eggs
225ml milk
75g unsalted butter, melted
225g Caerphilly, crumbled
8 spring onions, trimmed and thinly sliced
1 teaspoon finely chopped medium-hot
   red chilli
1 teaspoon extra virgin olive oil

Preheat the oven to 200°C fan/210°C/gas mark 7, and arrange 12 paper muffin cases inside a muffin tin rack. Combine the flour, cornmeal, grated pecorino, baking powder and salt in a large bowl. Whisk the eggs and milk in another large bowl, then stir in the melted butter. Pour this mixture onto the dry ingredients and blend to a lumpy batter. Fold in 150g of the Caerphilly, three quarters of the spring onions and the chilli and fill the paper cases to within 1cm of the top.

Toss the reserved spring onion with the olive oil and scatter this over the top of the muffins, then scatter over the rest of the Caerphilly. Bake for 10 minutes, then turn the oven down to 170°C fan/180°C/gas mark 5 and bake for another 15 minutes. Serve them warm or newly cooled.

SCOTCH EGG PIE

This halfway house between a pork pie and a Scotch egg avoids the fiddly bits involved in both.

For 6–8 people/Makes 1 x 22cm terrine

Pastry
450g plain flour
125g unsalted butter, chilled and diced, plus extra
   for greasing the tin
125g lard, chilled and diced
1 medium egg yolk
milk or water
Filling
6 medium eggs

800g meaty pork sausages, eg Toulouse
1 level tablespoon finely chopped rosemary
1 level tablespoon finely chopped sage
1 banana or 2 round shallots, peeled and finely
   chopped
sea salt and black pepper
1 tablespoon Dijon mustard
1 egg yolk blended with 1 tablespoon milk
   (eggwash)

To make the pastry place the flour, butter and lard in a food-processor, give it a quick burst at high speed to reduce it to a crumb-like consistency. Add the egg yolk and enough milk or water to bring the dough together, wrap it in clingfilm and chill for 1 hour or overnight. In the meantime, bring a medium pan of water to the boil, and simmer the eggs for 7 minutes. Drain the water, refill with cold and leave to cool.

 Preheat the oven to 170°C fan/180°C/gas mark 5. Grease and line the base and long sides of a 22cm (1.3-litre) loaf tin with baking paper, leaving it overhanging the sides. Now cut a long strip to line the base and ends, again so that it overhangs. Slit the sausages and slip the meat into a large bowl, then add the herbs, the shallots and some seasoning and work with your hands or a spoon until evenly blended. Shell the eggs and cut off the ends of white to just reveal the yolk.

Roll out two thirds of the pastry to 3–5mm thick on a lightly floured work surface, in a rectangular shape large enough to line the base and sides of the tin, with some overhanging, and lay it in place. Trim any excess leaving a couple of centimetres leeway, and roll these out with the remaining third of the pastry large enough to form a lid. Press about a third of the sausagemeat into the tin, then make a shallow trough down the centre and lay the eggs with each yolk touching the next in a line along the middle. Fill with the remaining sausagemeat, pressing it well down. Brush the mustard over the top of the sausagemeat, brush the pastry edges with eggwash and lay the rolled sheet of pastry on top, pressing the edges together well to seal the pie, then trim level with the tin. Brush the surface with the eggwash, make a few slits in the top and bake for 1½ hours.

Remove and leave to cool for 30 minutes, then carefully loosen the pie by lifting it a little way out of the tin using the paper overhang, and then letting it settle back again. Leave to cool and then chill, preferably overnight, before carefully lifting out and gently peeling off the paper – I would recommend transporting it in its tin, paper and all, although you could also cut and lay it out on a large serving plate.

Kit Serrated knife, plate

SIMPLE SPANISH TORTILLA

I don't think you can beat the austerity of a classic potato and onion tortilla. A humble basic but so delicious, you don't have to run to the Parmesan and herbs if you want something truly plain, it will still prove to take the starring role.

For 4–6 people

extra virgin olive oil
500g medium waxy potatoes, peeled or
   scrubbed as necessary and thickly sliced
sea salt and black pepper

100ml water
2 onions, peeled, halved and finely sliced
6 medium eggs
25g finely sliced Parmesan (optional)
2 tablespoons marjoram leaves (optional)

Heat 2 tablespoons of extra virgin olive oil in a 24cm non-stick frying pan with a heatproof handle over a medium heat, add the potatoes and cook them for about 5 minutes, turning them now and again, until they are coated in the oil. Season them with salt, add 100ml of water to the pan, cover it with a large saucepan lid and cook over a low heat for about 10 minutes until the potatoes are just tender. Using the lid, drain off any excess water and carefully transfer the potatoes to a large bowl.

Wipe the pan out with kitchen paper, return it to a medium heat, add another couple of tablespoons of oil and fry the onions for 7–10 minutes until golden, stirring frequently and seasoning them at the end. Mix them into the potatoes.

To cook the omelette, whisk the eggs in a bowl with a little seasoning, then pour them onto the potatoes and onions and gently stir to combine. Preheat the grill to high, and pop the frying pan in which you cooked the vegetables over a medium heat. Add a tablespoon of oil to the pan, tip in the egg and potato mixture, level the surface and cook for 3 minutes. Scatter the Parmesan slices over the top of the omelette, and then the marjoram leaves, if including. Drizzle over another tablespoon of oil and place under the grill for 3 minutes until golden and sizzling. It should still be slightly moist in the centre, but will firm up as it cools.

Kit Sharp knife, plate

ASPARAGUS AND SMOKED SALMON FRITTATA

This is a lively take on an omelette; the lemon, chilli and parsley together give the traditional duo of asparagus and smoked salmon a little warm weather appeal.

For 4 people

200g finger-thick asparagus, trimmed weight
6 medium eggs
½ teaspoon finely grated lemon zest, plus
  1 tablespoon lemon juice

2 teaspoons finely chopped medium-hot red chilli
4 tablespoons coarsely chopped flat-leaf parsley
100g sliced smoked salmon, brown meat cut off,
  and cut into strips 3–4cm wide
2 tablespoons extra virgin olive oil

Bring a large pan of salted water to the boil, and simmer the asparagus spears for 4–5 minutes until just tender, then drain them in a colander and pass them under a cold tap to stop them cooking any further.

Whisk the eggs in a large bowl, then whisk in the lemon zest and juice, the chilli and 3 tablespoons of parsley. Gently mix in the salmon and the asparagus spears.

Preheat the grill to high, and also put a 24cm frying pan with a heatproof handle over a medium heat. Add a tablespoon of oil to the pan, tip in the frittata mixture, levelling the asparagus, and cook for 3 minutes. Scatter the remaining parsley over the top of the omelette, drizzle over another tablespoon of oil and place under the grill for 3–4 minutes until golden and puffy at the sides.

Kit Sharp knife, plate

PASTA TIMBALE WITH LEEKS AND GOAT'S CHEESE

A great veggie main that makes a change from a savoury tart or omelette. This is good made with those slightly butch pastas that look as though they were made for Desperate Dan and might dwarf any sauce you put their way, tubular ones especially provide a welcome structure for the pie.

For 6 people

250g tortiglioni
extra virgin olive oil
3 leeks, trimmed and sliced
sea salt and black pepper
3 garlic cloves, peeled and finely chopped
2 tablespoons lemon thyme leaves

100g freshly grated Parmesan
3 medium eggs, plus 1 egg yolk
300ml whipping cream
150ml milk
200g medium-mature goat's cheese (weight excluding rind), cut into 1cm dice
6 tablespoons coarsely chopped flat-leaf parsley

Preheat the oven to 180°C fan/190°C/gas mark 6. Bring a large pan of salted water to the boil, add the tortiglioni, give it a stir and cook for about two thirds of the recommended time, then drain into a colander, return to the pan and toss with a slug of olive oil.

At the same time, heat a couple of tablespoons of oil in a large frying pan over a medium heat, add the leeks, season and fry for 5–7 minutes until they have started to soften and are lightly coloured, adding the garlic and half the thyme just before the end.

Brush a tablespoon of oil over the base of a 20cm cake tin 7cm deep, with a tightly fitting but removable collar, and scatter over a couple of tablespoons of Parmesan. Now whisk the eggs and yolk, cream, milk and some seasoning in a large bowl. Reserving a couple of tablespoons of the Parmesan, mix in the remainder. Fold in the leeks, pasta, two thirds of the goat's cheese and the parsley.

Place the tin on a baking sheet, fill with the mixture, and press down with your hands so that the ingredients are level and as far as possible submerged. Scatter over the remaining Parmesan, goat's cheese and thyme. Drizzle over another tablespoon of oil and bake for 45–50 minutes until set and golden, and there is no evidence of liquid in the centre if you pierce it with a knife.

Leave to cool. It is at its best eaten freshly cool, but can also be covered and chilled, in which case bring it back up to room temperature before serving.

Kit Sharp knife, plate, knife and fork

PEA TART 'À LA FRANÇAISE'

Of all the alternatives to a Quiche Lorraine, I find that a pea tart is the one that seems to go down best, not least because children love it. Do cheat and buy in the pastry if time is tight, but ideally all-butter.

For 6 people

Pastry
225g plain flour
a pinch of sea salt
150g unsalted butter, chilled and diced
1 medium egg, separated
cold water
Filling
25g unsalted butter
½ teaspoon caster sugar

sea salt and black pepper
400g fresh shelled peas
2 bunches spring onions (approx. 130g each), trimmed and sliced
1 Little Gem lettuce heart, thinly sliced
300ml whipping cream
2 medium eggs, plus 1 yolk
a handful of mint leaves, torn (optional)
150g freshly grated Parmesan

Place the flour and salt in the bowl of a food-processor, add the butter and reduce to a fine crumb-like consistency. Incorporate the egg yolk and then, with the motor running, trickle in just enough cold water for the dough to cling together into lumps. Wrap the pastry in clingfilm and chill for at least 1 hour.

Preheat the oven to 180°C fan/190°C/gas mark 6. Knead the pastry until it is pliable. Thinly roll it out on a lightly floured surface and carefully lift it into a 23cm tart tin 6cm deep with a removable base, pressing it into the corners of the tin and running a rolling pin over the top to trim the edges. Reserve the trimmings. Prick the base with a fork and line it with a sheet of foil, tucking it over the top to secure the pastry sides to the tin. Now weight it down with baking beans – dried pulses will do nicely.

Bake the case for 15 minutes, then remove the foil and baking beans. If any of the sides have shrunk more than they should, use a little of the reserved pastry to patch them. Brush the base and sides of the case with the reserved egg white, then bake it for another 10 minutes until it is lightly coloured.

In the meantime, place 150ml water in a large saucepan with the butter, sugar and ½ teaspoon of salt. Bring to the boil over a high heat, add the peas and cook for 5 minutes, stirring occasionally, until tender. Drain them into a sieve.

Reserving a couple of tablespoons of the spring onions, place the remainder in a small saucepan with the lettuce, the cream and some seasoning. Bring to the boil, cover with a lid, leaving a gap for the steam to escape, and simmer for 5 minutes. Whisk the eggs and yolk in a large bowl, then whisk in the cream and onion mixture, and fold in the peas, the mint, if including, and half the Parmesan. Transfer the filling to the tart case and scatter over the remaining Parmesan and the spring onions. Bake the tart on a preheated baking tray for 35–40 minutes until golden and set in the centre. Transport in the tin.

Kit Sharp knife, plate

CHERRY TOMATO AND PARMESAN GALETTES

Pizza-like in their appeal, children are unlikely to notice the crust is that little bit more delicate. These are just the right size for one per person, but cut up are also good as a communal offering to hand round.

For 6 people

300g puff pastry
Dijon mustard
300g cherry tomatoes, halved

1 medium egg yolk blended with 1 tablespoon
    water (eggwash)
sea salt and black pepper
30g finely shaved Parmesan
extra virgin olive oil

Preheat the oven to 200°C fan/210°C/gas mark 7. Thinly roll out the pastry on a lightly floured work surface – you can do this half at a time if it's easier – and cut out 6 x 12cm circles using a bowl or plate as a guide. Arrange these on a couple of baking sheets.

Spread a little Dijon mustard in the centre of each circle, to within about 2cm of the rim. Place the tomatoes on top. Brush the surrounding rim with the eggwash, then season the tomatoes, cover with a few slivers of Parmesan, drizzle over a little olive oil and bake for 15–20 minutes until golden and risen.

SALADS

Some years ago my husband and I

were on a trip to California, to visit the wonderful varietal garden attached to the Fetzer vineyards in Hopland, Mendocino County, to the north of San Francisco. Being rather green to the culture of Highway 101, we arrived there late afternoon devoid of any provisions. We were staying within the grounds of the garden, but hadn't realised there was nothing for miles around save a small general store close to the gates that didn't stock much more than popcorn and tinned tuna, and it had closed in any case. So we found ourselves, shut into the garden of paradise as the sun went down, with row upon row of wonderful ripe heirloom tomatoes, a fridge of delicious Fetzer wines to choose from, and a pot of salt and some oil in the cupboard, and that was it. By the time we went to bed I felt like Peter Rabbit locked into Mr McGregor's garden overnight, drunk on carrot juice, or a wasp trapped in a jam factory. But it was one of the most memorable feasts I can recall.

A couple of beautiful, ripe beefsteak tomatoes is still my idea of plenty on a picnic. Or I might take some tightly closed heads of chicory, or Little Gem hearts, by way of something green and leafy for dipping into the juices turning to jelly below the roast chicken in its foil. And if I do want to ratchet it up, then the classics of potato salad and coleslaw are classics for a reason, they jostle with all those cold cuts, pies and the like with just the right kind of informality.

Though one other ruse, for when you want to take either an all-in-one or something that little bit more sophisticated, is the layered salad. Here by arranging the dressing, and slighty heavier ingredients in the base of the dish, and working up to the leafier and more delicate ones, you can assemble everything you might want on your picnic in a single bowl, and simply toss it before eating. Perfect for that snatched interval at an outdoor opera or school sports day.

'A couple of beautiful, ripe beefsteak tomatoes is
my idea of plenty on a picnic.'

LET'S GO: CRUDITÉS

Raw slivers of vegetables often fare better than delicate salad leaves. Middle Eastern restaurants make a virtue out of the simplicity of crudités, flatbreads, a small saucer of oil for dipping and another of sea salt. While the Italians refer to the dipping of raw vegetables into olive oil and then salt as 'pinzimonio'.

For a picnic, crudités do away with the need for a salad, so they're a great last-minute solution that you can add to with dips, cheeses, pâté and cold meats. A few carefully chosen and prepared vegetables adds an essential homemade touch.

Trim and wash crudités before leaving and transport in an airtight container, in water with ice-cubes for maximum freshness if there is likely to be any substantial length of time before you eat them. You can take some unbreakable tumblers to arrange them in, or lightweight bowls. Also, take parsley, olive oil, a sachet of sea salt – you can twist this up in a piece of baking paper, and some bread.

TOMATOES

A couple of big, misshapen beefsteak tomatoes and a sachet of sea salt, provides one of the great rustic solutions on a picnic. Hack it into wedges for eating with a cold roast chicken, or slices of honey-roast ham and runny cheeses.

Otherwise a punnet of cherry tomatoes can be the starting point for a selection of crudités, if it's just two of you then look for a mixed punnet. While for any number of people a number of different punnets of cherry tomatoes or other varieties will make a big splash – baby plum tomatoes, cocktail cherry ones, red, yellow and orange, on the vine and off.

RADISHES

Long breakfast radishes are especially good. Give the bunch a good wash under the cold tap before leaving home and simply trim them once you get there.

RED AND YELLOW PEPPERS

Strips of pepper make for sweet and tender eating. Cut these as close to the time of eating as possible so they are crisp and fresh.

CELERY HEARTS

The heart of any head of celery has the most pronounced flavour and promises to be tender too. The stalk's naturally curved shape can support all manner of dips.

SPRING ONIONS

The slim ones are best for munching with cheese and cold meats, so trim them just before leaving home.

BABY CARROTS

Trim the stalk ends and peel if necessary, depending on their size.

A CRISP GREEN SALAD

With a little strategic thinking, some of the simplest salads are also the best, and can be assembled once you arrive at your destination. Be selective about the leaves, with the right frills or extras, and a two-ingredient dressing whisked up before you go, and you'll have a salad that will far outstrip any ready-made offering.

CHOOSING SALAD LEAVES

The original bags of **mixed salad leaves**, pioneered by the French co-operative Florette, are still a fine convenience. The down-side to this genre are many of the copy-cat bags that include parts of the leaf that we would rather not be eating, or they are tired, whereby the convenience turns into the inconvenience of having to sort through them and rid them of any browning parts.

Single leaves tend to fare better than mixed (at least they wilt at the same rate), so you can tell by looking at them whether or not they are fresh. A bag of **watercress**, **rocket** or a punnet of **mustard and cress** are all good choices. Beyond this, young tightly closed heads of lettuce such as **Little Gem and Romaine hearts**, and heads of **Belgian chicory** need only have the base sliced off and the outer leaves discarded, before separating out the crisp and tender leaves within. I love munching on **flat-leaf parsley** in the company of salty cold cuts, or with a sliver of cheese and chutney, it provides a breath of fresh air, clean and sweet.

Floppy round lettuces can also be put to good use. Discard any leathery outer leaves, and give the lettuce a good rinse under the cold tap, then shake dry. Twist off the base, and place whole in a cupped bowl, then loosen the leaves as though you were opening out a flower, and scatter over some **snipped chives**. Drizzle over a **vinaigrette** to serve.
Allow one for 2–4 people

SALAD DRESSINGS

When it comes to salad dressings, there's no need to run to more than two ingredients, or four if you count the salt and pepper. Blend it before leaving and have it ready in a small clip-top storage container or empty jam jar.

Vinaigrette dressing

Shake a tablespoon of **balsamic vinegar or lemon juice** with some **sea salt** and ground **black pepper** in a small clip-top container or jar. Add 3 tablespoons of **extra virgin olive oil** and shake again. Or, for something slightly more exotic, you could extend this to a t**omato, passionfruit or fig vinegar**, for instance, and a **walnut or hazelnut oil**.
For 6 people

Creamy Mustard Dressing

Blend 150ml **soured cream** with 2 heaped teaspoons of **Dijon mustard**, a generous pinch of **caster sugar** and a little **sea salt** and chill.
For 6 people

Cheat's Mayonnaise

Blend 3 tablespoons of **mayonnaise** and 3 tablespoons of **soured cream**, a little **caster sugar** and **sea salt**.
For 6 people

SALAD EXTRAS

● Pine nuts, toasted or untoasted ● Pumpkin seeds ● Macadamia nuts ● Roasted salted cashews ● Roasted salted almonds ● Green or black olives, marinated or stuffed ● Herb leaves – mint, flat-leaf parsley, dill ● Cherry tomatoes ● Diced feta ● Parmesan shavings

PICNIC COLESLAW

I only have to see pictures of July 4th picnics and the Stars and Stripes to think 'coleslaw'. And why not? It's easy to see why a big, creamy bowl of the stuff is a staple, it travels like a pro and all that dressing is great with cold roast chicken, sausages and the like. Refinement in a coleslaw rests with slicing that butch head of cabbage wafer fine, so sharpen up the knives.

For 6 people

125g Greek yogurt
60g mayonnaise
½ tablespoon white wine or tarragon vinegar
½ tablespoon caster sugar
sea salt
½ small Savoy cabbage
2 slim carrots, peeled and finely sliced diagonally
3 slim spring onions, trimmed and finely sliced
2 stalks of celery heart, finely sliced
50g chopped walnuts (optional)

Blend the yogurt, mayonnaise, vinegar, sugar and a little salt in a large bowl. Quarter the cabbage, cut out the core and slice wafer thin, then halve the strands. Reserving a little of the carrot and a third of the spring onion, toss the remainder into the dressing along with the cabbage, celery and walnuts, if including. Spoon into a transportable container or serving bowl, and scatter over the reserved carrot and spring onion.

Kit Serving spoon, plate, fork

NEW POTATO, ROASTED RED ONION AND CASHEW SALAD

This is one step up in sophistication from the potato salad on page 86, more in line with the boutique patisserie fare we have come to love. It's worth taking any leftover salad back home with you, as it can be sliced and sautéed or made into a tortilla a day or so later.

For 6 people

1.2kg small new potatoes, unpeeled, scrubbed if necessary
6 tablespoons extra virgin olive oil
2 tablespoons dry vermouth or white wine
sea salt and black pepper

4 red onions, peeled, halved and thinly sliced
2 tablespoons tarragon leaves
3 tablespoons snipped chives
100g roasted cashew nuts (whole)

Preheat the oven to 180°C fan/190°C/gas mark 6. Meanwhile, bring a large pan of salted water to the boil. Halve any large potatoes, so they are all roughly the same size, add to the pan and boil for 20–25 minutes until tender, then drain them in a sieve and leave for a few minutes for the surface moisture to evaporate. Transfer them to a large bowl and toss with 4 tablespoons of olive oil, the vermouth and some seasoning, and leave to cool.

At the same time as the potatoes are cooking, toss the onions in a bowl with 2 tablespoons of oil and spread them out in a thin layer on a couple of baking sheets. Roast for 20–25 minutes until golden, giving them a stir halfway through to ensure they colour evenly. Leave to cool.

Toss the roasted onion, herbs and nuts into the potatoes before leaving.

Kit Serving spoon, plate, fork

DELI COUNTER POTATO SALAD

A great basic. Here, a little soured cream in with some bottled mayo softens the edges, and fresh parsley works wonders to bring it to life. Yummy with roast chicken, tail-on cooked prawns and lightly boiled eggs (hen's 7–8 minutes or quail's 2½ minutes).

For 4 people

750g small waxy potatoes, peeled or scrubbed
Dressing
100g soured cream
100g mayonnaise
sea salt
1 tablespoon finely chopped shallot

2 tablespoons small capers (such as
    nonpareille), rinsed
2 tablespoons finely chopped flat-leaf parsley,
    plus extra to serve
cayenne pepper (optional)

Bring a large pan of salted water to the boil, add the potatoes and cook until tender, then drain in a colander. Leave to cool and then dice.

Blend the soured cream and mayonnaise in a bowl with a pinch of salt. Stir in the shallot, capers and parsley, and then the potatoes. Transfer to a transportable bowl or container. Dust with cayenne pepper, if wished, and scatter over some more parsley.

Kit Serving spoon, plate, fork

QUINOA TABBOULEH

Quinoa makes for an almost better picnic tabbouleh than bulgar wheat, lusciously soft and comforting, this salad can stand in for potato or pasta while being every bit as vibrant and lively as the Middle Eastern classic. You'll need nice big bunches of herbs for this, just the tender young leaves. And as ever you want really good tomatoes; they don't have to be cherry, any type that promise to be sweet and juicy will do the trick. You could also stir some diced feta into the salad at the very end, about 200g cut into 1cm dice.

For 4–6 people

200g quinoa
3 tablespoons lemon juice
2 tablespoons water
sea salt and black pepper
8 tablespoons extra virgin olive oil

15g young mint leaves, coarsely chopped
75g young flat-leaf parsley leaves, coarsely chopped
250g cherry tomatoes, halved or quartered depending on their size
6 spring onions, trimmed and thinly sliced

Bring a medium pan of salted water to the boil. Heat a large frying pan over a medium heat, scatter the quinoa over the base and toast for a few minutes, stirring frequently, until it gives off a lovely warming aroma and starts popping. Transfer to a bowl and leave to cool for a few minutes, then add to the boiling water and simmer for 15–20 minutes until tender. Drain through a sieve, return it to the saucepan, cover and leave to cool.

Whisk the lemon juice with the water and some seasoning in a small airtight container, then whisk in the oil. Combine the herbs in a large bowl or container with the tomatoes, onions and quinoa. You can prepare the salad to this point up to a couple of hours in advance, in which case cover and take the dressing separately, and pour this over and mix at the time.

Kit Serving spoon, plate, fork

PESTO MACARONI SALAD

A layered salad with a zesty pesto dressing and cherry tomatoes, that also doubles as a hot pasta dish with a minute or two's warming in a saucepan over a gas flame if you are in need of something warming on a picnic (see pages 120–143). Essentially it takes no time at all to prepare, but it is worth investing in a decent jar of pesto. (For 4–6 people, scale it down to 200g pasta, 350g tomatoes, 5 tablespoons of olive oil and 2 of pesto, respectively.)

For 6–8 people

300g macaroni or penne
7 tablespoons extra virgin olive oil
sea salt and black pepper
400–450g baby plum or mixed cherry tomatoes,
    halved
3 tablespoons pesto
a couple of handfuls of coarsely chopped
    flat-leaf parsley

Bring a large pan of salted water to the boil, add the macaroni, give it a stir and cook until just tender. Drain in a colander, briefly run under the cold tap to stop any further cooking, then toss with a tablespoon of oil in a bowl and leave to cool. At the same time, season the tomatoes with salt in another bowl and set aside for 15–30 minutes.

Whisk the pesto, remaining oil and a little seasoning in a large serving bowl. Scatter the tomatoes on top, drizzling over any juices given out, then scatter over the pasta and, finally, the parsley. Toss to serve when you're ready to eat.

Kit Serving spoon, plate, fork

PEA AND MINT SALAD

These veg will happily sit for days in the fridge, drinking up the garlic and mint, as long as you season them with lemon at the last minute.

For 4–6 people

350g fresh shelled peas
250g mangetouts, stalk-end trimmed
250g sugarsnaps, topped and tailed
2–3 garlic cloves, peeled and crushed to a paste
2 shallots, peeled and finely chopped
4 strips of lemon zest
9 tablespoons extra virgin olive oil
a couple of large handfuls of mint leaves, coarsely chopped
1 tablespoon sesame seeds
sea salt and black pepper
a couple of squeezes of lemon juice

Bring a large pan of salted water to the boil. Add the peas and cook for 3 minutes, adding the mangetouts and sugarsnaps after 2 minutes. Drain the vegetables into a colander and refresh them under the cold tap, then set aside for a few minutes for the surface moisture to evaporate.

Mix the garlic, shallot, lemon zest and olive oil in a large bowl, add the cooked vegetables and toss to coat them. Leave to cool, then mix in the mint and seeds. Cover and chill overnight, or longer if you want, though equally you can eat the salad straightaway.

Discard the lemon zest and season with salt and pepper before leaving home, and take a lemon with you to squeeze over just before serving.

Kit Serving spoon, plate, fork

CHERRY TOMATO SALAD

A simple tomato salad, like a potato salad, is a wonderful picnic basic. This lively rendition lends itself in particular to the Middle Eastern palate, so think hummus and olives, pickled chillies and salty sheep's cheeses. On the same note, you can make a salad of sliced **tomatoes** with a drizzle of **extra virgin olive oil**, a sprinkling of **sea salt** and a fine dusting of **ground sumac**, the sharp-tasting rust-red berries. Or sprinkle over **za'atar**, a blend of ground sesame seeds, dried thyme, sumac and sea salt. Failing this **dried oregano or mint** is ever a delicious touch.

For 4 people

600g mixed cherry tomatoes, halved or quartered, depending on size
caster sugar
sea salt
4 tablespoons extra virgin olive oil
2 tablespoons lemon juice
1 large shallot, peeled, halved and finely chopped
4 tablespoons coarsely chopped flat-leaf parsley

Toss the tomatoes with a little sugar and salt in a bowl or other container and set aside for 15–30 minutes. Pour over the olive oil and lemon juice, then scatter over the shallot and parsley and gently toss.

Kit Serving spoon, plate, fork

CUCUMBER, CHILLI AND PUMPKIN SEED SALAD

This has a clean, gazpacho-like charm, laced with chilli, spring onions and lemon, it would be lovely with Gravadlax (see page 45), Poolside Prawns (see page 140) or the Grand Salmon (see page 119). There is no need to peel the cucumbers here, the salt works its magic on the skin that ends up as tender as the inside, with just a little crunch.

For 6–8 people

2 cucumbers, ends discarded, halved,
   deseeded and sliced into half moons
   about 3mm thick
sea salt
50g pumpkin seeds or pine nuts
4 tablespoons extra virgin olive oil
2 tablespoons lemon juice
3 spring onions, trimmed and finely sliced
½ medium-hot red chilli, seeds discarded and
   finely chopped
1 handful of coarsely chopped coriander

Season the cucumber with sea salt in a large bowl and set aside for 30 minutes. Give the cucumber a good rinse in a sieve or a sink of cold water, then dry it in batches between double thicknesses of kitchen paper. At the same time, heat a frying pan over a medium heat and toast the pumpkin seeds or pine nuts until lightly coloured, stirring constantly, then transfer them to a bowl and leave to cool.

Combine the oil and lemon juice in a serving bowl or sealable container. Scatter the cucumber on top of the salad, then the spring onion, chilli, coriander and seeds, and cover to transport. Toss the salad in the dressing just before serving.

Kit Serving spoon, plate, fork

GRILLED BROCCOLI AND SESAME SALAD

Long-stemmed broccoli has replaced asparagus in my affections, and grilling renders it sweet but with a delicious faint bitterness. These spears are great finger food but also make a good basic that can be dressed up. Beyond sesame seeds, which are an instant finishing touch, maybe turn it into a salad with strips of Medjool dates and ripe tomatoes, or add some cooked broad beans, pine nuts and the like. You can forego the sesame seeds, if you prefer, and simply grill the broccoli with olive oil.

For 4 people

400g tenderstem broccoli, trimmed
1 tablespoon sesame seeds
2 tablespoons groundnut or vegetable oil

2 teaspoons sesame oil
sea salt and black pepper

Bring a large pan of salted water to the boil, add the broccoli and cook for 3 minutes, then drain in a colander and leave for a few minutes for the surface moisture to evaporate. Toast the sesame seeds in a small frying pan over a medium heat until lightly coloured, stirring constantly, then transfer to a bowl and leave to cool.

Heat a ridged griddle over a medium heat. Blend the groundnut and sesame oil, pour this over the broccoli in a bowl and toss, then season. Grill in two to three batches for 2–3 minutes each side until golden or charred, arranging the spears on a plate or in a container as you go. Scatter over the sesame seeds.

Kit Serving spoon, plate

OVEN-ROAST RATATOUILLE

I turn to this again and again during the summer as my default way of cooking ratatouille. Not only do the vegetables concentrate in flavour in the oven, but also there is no frying or hovering over a hot pan, the last thing you want in serious heat. As ever this is a building block, it goes beautifully with fine shavings of Tomme de Savoie cheese, olives and cured meats. And it's good for making the night before.

For 6 people

1kg beefsteak tomatoes, halved through
   the core
approx. 500g aubergines, stalk-ends trimmed,
   halved lengthways (or quartered if large)
   and thickly sliced
extra virgin olive oil
4 red peppers, core and seeds removed and
   thinly sliced lengthways
approx. 500g courgettes, ends trimmed, halved
   lengthways if large, and thickly sliced
sea salt and black pepper
3 red onions, peeled, halved and sliced
4 garlic cloves, peeled and thinly sliced
a handful of coarsely chopped curly or
   flat-leaf parsley

Preheat the oven to 200°C fan/210°C/gas mark 7. You will need three good-sized roasting dishes that will fit in the oven together. Arrange the tomatoes cut-side up in a tightly fitting single layer in one. Brush the aubergine with oil on both sides and arrange with the peppers and courgettes in another couple of roasting dishes in a crowded layer, they will shrink as they cook. Drizzle a couple of tablespoons of oil over the tomatoes, and about 6 tablespoons over the other veg and season everything.

Roast all three dishes for 1–1¼ hours, stirring the onions and garlic into the peppers and courgettes after 30 minutes. Gently stir or turn them again 15 minutes later, concealing any well-coloured vegetables below the surface, and continue to roast until well-coloured. Leave all the vegetables to cool.

Remove the skin from the tomatoes and nick out the hard core, then coarsely chop using a knife and fork. Combine all the vegetables, including the chopped tomatoes, in a sealable bowl or container, to transport, gently folding in the parsley just before serving.

Kit Serving spoon, plate, fork

SLOW-ROAST TOMATOES

Just occasionally, and delightfully, work lands me on an elegant picnic somewhere exotic. One such occasion was in the South of France, outside St Tropez in the shade of a vine, where lunch took the form of a beautiful selection of goat's cheeses from the local market, a big rocket salad dressed with extra virgin olive oil and lemon juice, a large Le Parfait jar of slowly roasted tomatoes and some sourdough bread. All told there was very little preparation involved, save the tomatoes that can be made well in advance, on a quiet midweek evening with the weekend in mind.

I've played with slow-roasting tomatoes endlessly over the years, and settled on this as the best method. There is no skinning or fiddly preparation, just small sweet tomatoes rendered even sweeter after a couple of hours in a slow oven. But it's difficult to be too exact with timings – it will depend on the size of the tomatoes, how juicy they are and how many you are cooking – so keep a watchful eye.

For 6 people/makes approx. 300g

600g cherry or cocktail tomatoes on the vine,
    halved
4 garlic cloves, skin-on and crushed
5 sprigs of thyme
sea salt
caster sugar
extra virgin olive oil

Preheat the oven to 120°C fan/130°C/gas mark 1½. Lay the tomato halves skin-downwards in a single layer in a roasting tray lined with baking paper. Scatter over the garlic and the thyme, pulling off half the leaves, and season with salt and a sprinkling of sugar. Drizzle over 3 tablespoons of olive oil and bake them for 1¾–2½ hours; until they are semi-dry, concentrated in flavour but retaining some succulence, they will reduce by about half their weight. Leave to cool.

If not serving straightaway, place them in a bowl or a jar and cover with olive oil. Chill for up to 3 days, bringing back up to room temperature before serving.

Kit Serving spoon, plate

ROASTED RED PEPPER AND LENTIL SALAD

I used to cook this endlessly in the 1980s. Lentils and roasted peppers make a charmed marriage, especially good with goat's cheese, olives and salami. Should you want to take some roasted peppers on their own, then simply omit the lentils. This good-natured salad can be made several hours in advance and it will play happily to a mixed crowd of carnivores and vegetarians.

For 6 people

6 red peppers, core and seeds removed, and
 quartered lengthways
10–12 thyme sprigs
2 bay leaves
7 tablespoons extra virgin olive oil
sea salt and black pepper

1 head of garlic, cloves peeled
1 tablespoon balsamic vinegar
150g French lentils (such as Le Puy)
coarsely chopped flat-leaf parsley, to serve
 (optional)

Preheat the oven to 200°C fan/210°C/gas mark 7. Arrange the peppers in a crowded single layer in a large roasting dish and tuck the herbs between them. Drizzle over 4 tablespoons of oil and season with salt and pepper. Roast for 25 minutes, then scatter over the garlic cloves, baste everything and roast for another 15–25 minutes or until golden and nicely singed. When the vegetables come out of the oven, drizzle over the vinegar and leave to cool.

At the same time, bring a medium pan of water to the boil and cook the lentils for 15–25 minutes until tender but retaining their shape, then drain into a sieve, briefly run under the cold tap and leave to cool.

Scatter the lentils over the peppers (discarding the thyme and bay), drizzle over the remaining oil, season with a little more salt and gently toss. Scatter with parsley if wished, and cover to transport.

Kit Salad servers, plate, knife and fork

LAYERED NIÇOISE

I tend to return from France to London loaded with basics that I can't readily find once I am back. The checkout attendants at the local supermarket look at me curiously as they scan the twentieth bottle of Le Petit Marseillais shampoo, and the umpteenth tin of fish. There is a huge differential between indifferent and very good sardines in oil, and tuna in brine, and these are one of the basics of my storecupboard. Not that tinned fish cannot be found in most major cities thoughout the world, simply that Northern France and Spain make a delicacy out of this humble staple. The ideal for this salad, is a good meaty whole chunk of fish that can be broken into neat chunks or coarsely flaked, rather than something that is on its way to being a pâté before you have even spooned it out of the tin.

For 4 people

4 medium eggs
6 tablespoons extra virgin olive oil
1½ tablespoons lemon juice
sea salt and black pepper
2 tablespoons small capers, rinsed
2 x 200g jars or tins of tuna in oil or spring
  water, drained

4 salted anchovy fillets, halved lengthways
3 ripe plum or speciality tomatoes such as
  heirloom, cores cut out and cut into wedges
70g pitted green or black olives
70–80g rocket leaves

Bring a medium pan of water to the boil, add the eggs and boil for 7–8 minutes to leave them slightly moist in the centre, then drain and cool in cold water, shell them and halve.

Whisk the olive oil, the lemon juice, some seasoning and the capers in a large deep salad bowl, with room to spare for tossing once you have layered all the ingredients. Dry the tuna on a double thickness of kitchen paper, and break into chunks or coarsely flake. Add to the dressing, and turn to coat everything. Lay the anchovy fillets on top, then the tomatoes and scatter over the olives. Finally pile the rocket on top, and lay over the eggs.

Cover to transport and toss to serve once you are at the picnic.

Kit Serving spoon, plate, fork

COUSCOUS SALAD WITH PISTACHIOS AND POMEGRANATE

A couscous salad has become almost de rigueur on the picnic table. So much so that when a friend invited us to the opera at Glyndebourne this summer, with a 'bring a salad' tagged on, this seemed the obvious choice. The only snag being that he had made one too, so it was a 'couscous cook-off' as he put it, or something like turning up in the same dress. So, if you are going to provide a couscous salad, better make sure it's good, just in case.

For 6 people

250ml vegetable stock
sea salt
a pinch of saffron filaments (approx. 20)
200g couscous
seeds of 1 medium pomegranate
75g shelled pistachio nuts (roasted or unroasted)
6 tablespoons coarsely chopped coriander
6 tablespoons coarsely chopped mint
zest of 1 lemon, removed with a zester
1 tablespoon lemon juice
4 tablespoons extra virgin olive oil
pomegranate syrup, to serve (optional)

Bring the stock to the boil in a small saucepan, season with salt, if you wish, and add the saffron. Pour this over the couscous in a large bowl, cover and set aside for 30 minutes, stirring and breaking it up halfway through. Leave to cool completely.

Mix the pomegranate seeds, pistachios, herbs and lemon zest into the couscous. You can prepare the salad to this point in advance, and transport it in a sealed container. Whisk the lemon juice with the olive oil and some salt in a small sealable container to transport. At the picnic, pour the dressing over the salad, toss and drizzle with pomegranate syrup.

Kit Serving spoon, plate, fork

SUNDAY ROAST PICNIC

It's easy to picture rural scenes of

meadows and riverbanks when you think of a picnic, but cities offer myriad places too. Most cities around the world have parks – big open spaces landscaped for our pleasure, with grass just waiting for us to come along with a rug under our arm. In fact, because of the nature of land ownership in some countries, urban areas can offer many more opportunities for picnics and lovely walks than the countryside does. Whichever city of the world you happen to find yourself in, an escape from the hustle and bustle of the pavements is never far away.

So, this chapter lies particularly close to my heart, given how much time we spend in London. In fact, this is my Hyde Park ideal, being able to spread yourself on rugs in the shade of a plane tree somewhere between the Round Pound and the Serpentine and you have an afternoon of hippy nirvana without leaving town. Opening up a foil package with a roast chicken still slightly warm from the oven, for eating with some crisp green leaves and a loaf of coarsely torn sourdough bread or a baguette and it is about as close as it gets to heaven in my book.

In fact, a Sunday roast picnic is rather easier than going the whole hog of a roast lunch at home, where there are all those trimmings to consider and pans to wash up at the end. Come the summer we can forego all of that and turn to relaxed Mediterranean flavours and vegetables, with bread taking the place of potatoes. The idea is to get roasting while packing (or the other way around), then whisk your chicken, leg of lamb or the like straight from the oven, wrapped in its foil overcoat, hot to your destination, where it will still have that gorgeous ambient succulence that belongs to meat by rights before it has been cooled or chilled.

There is something deliciously decadent about eating slightly warm or freshly cooked food out of doors, just as swimming in a steaming hot swimming pool in the freezing cold has an air of being exotic, removed from their normal setting the humblest of roasts seems special.

Getting in there with your fingers adds to the charm, lovely messy rusticity, so I wouldn't even think knife and fork here. The pan juices are at the ready for mopping up with a hunk of bread – a twenty-first century tale of bread and dripping, something my mother's generation regarded as a treat long after the war was over and butter was back on the menu.

'There is something deliciously decadent about eating slightly warm or freshly cooked food out of doors.'

LET'S GO: ROASTS

As a last-minute solution to a picnic, I am more likely to roast a chicken or cook some sausages than anything else. Recently I had to put this to the ultimate test, when the chicken I had lined up for fifteen of us for a Sunday lunch picnic proved to be less than fresh on the morning. So, the challenge was to get to the shops, get home, roast a main dish and get to the picnic all in the space of an hour and a half. And it worked! A row of chooks roasted with ras al hanout were hot and on the rug in time. If you line the roasting tray with a double thickness of foil large enough to wrap the bird up in as it comes out of the oven, it should still be slightly warm a couple of hours later.

AROUND THE WORLD IN 80 SAUSAGES

I swear by roasting **sausages** in the oven, where they caramelise beautifully and evenly; in fact I cannot recall the last time I cooked one in a frying pan, too messy by half. Different types and sizes will inevitably differ marginally in the length of time they take to cook, but as a rule of thumb, lay them out in a roasting dish spaced slightly apart (you can brush it with **vegetable oil** first if wished, although I don't usually bother). Then roast for 35–40 minutes at 200°C fan/210°C/gas mark 7, turning them once with a spatula.

A SALT AND PEPPER BIRD

A salt and pepper bird is just that – a sprinkling of **sea salt** and grinding of **black pepper**, there is enough fat beneath the skin to baste it. Roast a **1.6kg free-range untrussed bird** for 50–55 minutes at 200°C fan/210°C/gas mark 7 until the skin is golden and the juices run clear when a knife is inserted into the thigh.

For 4–5 people

GARLIC AND THYME CHICKEN

Coat a **1.6kg free-range untrussed chicken** with **olive oil** and season it with **sea salt** and **black pepper**, pop some **thyme**, a smashed **garlic clove or two**, and **half an onion** into the cavity and roast as opposite.

For 4–5 people

BUTTER AND LEMON CHICKEN

Another favourite way is to dot a **1.6kg free-range untrussed chicken** with **unsalted butter**, squeeze over a little **lemon juice** (popping the squeezed-out lemon inside), season it well with **sea salt** and **black pepper** and roast as opposite.

For 4–5 people

SPICY ROAST CHICKEN

Blend 1 teaspoon of **ras al hanout or garam masala** with 1 tablespoon of **lemon juice** and 2 tablespoons of **olive oil** in a small bowl. Smear this over a **1.6kg free-range untrussed chicken** on a plate. If you like you can chill it for a couple of hours. Season with **sea salt** and **black pepper** and roast as opposite.

For 4–5 people

MY FAVOURITE PICNIC ROAST CHICKEN

This is my default bird, scented with resinous herbs and with lots of lemony juices to mop up with a hunk of bread or some green leaves.

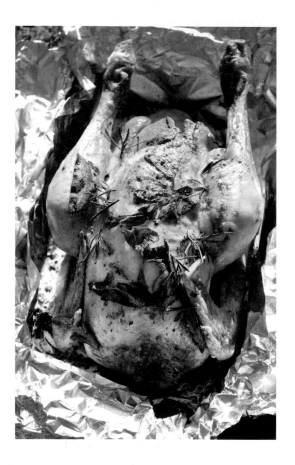

For 6 people

1 x approx. 2kg free-range chicken, untrussed
sea salt and black pepper
a large handful of sage leaves and a few
   rosemary sprigs
3 tablespoons extra virgin olive oil
1 lemon, halved

Preheat the oven to 200°C fan/210°C/gas mark 7. Place the chicken in a roasting dish lined with a double thickness of foil large enough to wrap the bird up in once cooked – depending on the width of the foil you may find it easiest to place the sheets at right angles to each other.

Season the chicken and scatter over the sage leaves and rosemary sprigs, first pulling off half the needles. Carefully drizzle over the oil taking care not to dislodge the herbs, squeeze over the juice of a lemon and pop the squeezed-out halves inside the chicken. Roast for 1 hour, then skim off the excess fat from the juices and wrap up in the foil to transport.

Kit Sharp knife, plate, knife and fork (optional)

GORGEOUSLY BUTTERY VERY FRENCH CHICKEN

The herbs that go to make up a classical French 'fines herbes' together form one of the quintessential scents of the cooking of this country. But finding fresh chervil? I confess that I have hardly ever seen it outside of doing time as a commis chef in a restaurant. There is no real substitute, but if needs must then mock up its gentle shades of tarragon in parsley with a little of the former and more of the latter – that is, a blend of tarragon, parsley and chives. Whatever route you choose – and you could even reduce it to parsley alone – this is still a brilliant way of cooking chicken, its flesh infused with buttery succulence and a rich skin.

For 4 people

5 tablespoons finely chopped herbs, such as
    chervil, tarragon, chives, parsley
75g unsalted butter, softened
sea salt and black pepper
1 x 1.6kg free-range chicken, untrussed

Preheat the oven to 200°C fan/210°C/gas mark 7. Blend the herbs with 50g of the butter and half a teaspoon each of salt and pepper in a bowl. Starting at the neck end of the chicken, slip your fingers beneath the skin to loosen it over each breast. Gently smooth the butter and herb mixture over the breasts and pat the skin back into place, spreading the butter out evenly. Rub the remaining butter over the chicken and season.

Place the chicken in a roasting dish that holds it quite snugly, lined with a double thickness of foil large enough to wrap the chicken up in – depending on the width of the foil you may find it easiest to place two sheets at right angles to each other. Roast for 50 minutes, then spoon off any excess fat in the base and wrap up in the foil to transport.

Kit Sharp knife, plate, knife and fork (optional)

CHICKEN TIKKA MASALA

Despite having to do a little cooking, this marinade won't take more than 10 minutes to make. It can be whizzed up the night before and the chicken left to marinate, ready to cook before the off. One of the speedy dips, such as guacamole (see page 30) or tzatziki (see page 30) make a good aside here, or an aubergine or roasted pepper one. Alternatively, take a cucumber to slice when you get there for assembling tikka sarnies.

Makes 12 mini tikkas

6 skinless chicken breasts (approx. 700–800g)
Tikka marinade
groundnut or vegetable oil
1 onion, peeled and finely chopped
3 garlic cloves, peeled and crushed to a paste
5cm ginger root, peeled and grated or finely
  chopped
1 teaspoon yellow mustard seeds

½ teaspoon ground cumin or seeds
1 teaspoon garam masala
½ teaspoon cayenne pepper
100g tomato purée
sea salt
150ml coconut milk
coarsely chopped coriander, to serve

To make the marinade, heat a couple of tablespoons of oil in a large frying pan over a medium heat, add the onion and fry for a few minutes until softened and starting to colour, stirring occasionally. Add the garlic and ginger and cook for a minute or so longer, stirring frequently. Now stir in the spices and cook briefly until fragrant. Stir in the tomato purée, season with salt and cook for minute or so longer, then gradually stir in the coconut milk. Transfer the marinade to a large container and leave to cool. You can prepare this the night before your picnic.

Cut out the white tendon on the underside of each chicken breast if evident, and halve into two long strips. Coat the breasts with the marinade in the bowl, cover and chill or keep in a cool place for a couple of hours or overnight.

Heat a ridged griddle pan over a high heat. The chicken breasts should be lightly coated in the marinade. Drizzle a little oil over either side and grill for a few minutes each side until striped with gold, you can press down with spatula for this bit, and they should feel firm. Scatter with coriander before packaging to transport to your picnic.

Kit Plate, knife and fork

TRAYBAKE CHICKEN WITH ZA'ATAR AND PINE NUTS

You should end up here with a delectable pool of juices, sharpened with lemon and scented with cinnamon and the thyme of the za'atar (available mail order from www.seasonedpioneers.co.uk), although almost any Middle Eastern spice blend can be used, so tailor it to fit the storecupboard. The pine nuts and coriander are a frill, if I am catering for lots of children then I tend to leave these aside as an option for those that want.

For 6 people

2 lemons
150ml extra virgin olive oil
3 garlic cloves, peeled and crushed to a paste
1 red onion, peeled and finely chopped
2 heaped teaspoons za'atar
2 cinnamon sticks, broken in half
1.8–2kg chicken thighs and drumsticks
sea salt and black pepper
50g pine nuts (optional)
coriander leaves, to serve (optional)

Slice one of the lemons, discarding the ends, and juice the other. Combine the lemon juice and olive oil, garlic, onion, za'atar, cinnamon and sliced lemon in a large bowl. Add the chicken pieces to the bowl and coat with the marinade. Cover and chill for several hours.

Preheat the oven to 200°C fan/210°C/gas mark 7. Season the chicken pieces and arrange them skin-side up in a single layer in two roasting trays, drizzling over the marinade and tucking the lemon slices between them. Roast for 35 minutes until golden, scattering over the pine nuts, if including, after 15 minutes. Skim off the excess fat and pack to transport. A few coriander leaves scattered over before serving is a lively touch.

Kit Serving plate

MUSTARD ROAST GUINEA FOWL QUARTERS

Guinea fowl tend to come up that little bit smaller than chicken, which makes them good for eating in quarters. But they do call for a knife and fork, being that much firmer than a chook. If buying from a butcher then I would prevail upon them to cut the birds up for you, but otherwise it's a fairly straightforward task, but a strong pair of hands is required.

For 6 people

2 x 1.1–1.2kg guinea fowl, quartered
3 tablespoons cider vinegar
approx. 6 tablespoons groundnut oil
700g red onions, peeled and quartered or cut
   into slim wedges, depending on their size
approx. 10 bay leaves
sea salt and black pepper
1 tablespoon Dijon mustard
1 level tablespoon savory or thyme leaves

Place the guinea fowl pieces in a large bowl, pour over the vinegar and a couple of tablespoons of oil, cover and set aside in a cool place to marinate for an hour, or chill.

Preheat the oven to 200°C fan/210°C/gas mark 7. Arrange the guinea fowl pieces skin-side-up in two roasting dishes surrounded by the onions and bay leaves, so they sit in a crowded single layer. Pour the marinade over the contents, drizzle over another 2–3 tablespoons of oil, season and roast for 20 minutes.

Give the onions a stir, brush the guinea fowl pieces with the mustard and scatter over the savoury or thyme. Baste the meat with any juices and drizzle over another tablespoon or so of oil, then return to the oven for another 15–20 minutes. Pour off the juices, skim off the fat and serve the remainder drizzled over the guinea fowl and onions.

Kit Plate, knife and fork (optional)

LEG OF LAMB WITH ANCHOVIES

HERBED RACK OF LAMB

Roast lamb studded with anchovies is one of those strange but true combinations, where it brings out the sweetness of the flesh but there is no hint of the salty little fish, they simply melt away. A small leg weighing 1.6–1.7kg is perfect for four (although obviously you can roast a larger one).

Delicate pale pink chops are perfect for nibbling in hand at a slightly special picnic. Either slice them just before you go, and keep the rack together wrapped in foil, or, as they cut like butter, take a sharp folding knife and do it when you arrive at your picnic location.

For 4 people

1 x approx. 1.7kg leg of lamb, knuckle
   removed
4–5 salted anchovies, cut into 1cm nibs
extra virgin olive oil
sea salt and black pepper
a handful of thyme sprigs

For 6 people

sea salt and black pepper
2 x 500–700g racks of lamb
2 teaspoons wholegrain mustard
several handfuls each of sage and bay
   leaves, and rosemary sprigs
extra virgin olive oil

Preheat the oven to 230°C fan/240°C/gas mark 9. Using a sharp knife make slits all over the lamb flesh, and with the help of the tip of a teaspoon handle insert a nib of anchovy into each one. Drizzle some olive oil all over the lamb, season the joint and place fat-side up in a roasting tray that holds it snugly, on top of the thyme. You can also tuck the knuckle bone under the edge of the joint.

Roast for 15 minutes, then turn the oven down to 160°C fan/170°C/gas mark 4 and cook for a further 55 minutes (cook for 33 minutes per kg for medium). Wrap in foil and you're ready to go. Carve the lamb across the grain, you may prefer to do this just before you leave the house, in which case leave to rest for 15–20 minutes first.

Preheat the oven to 200°C fan/210°C/gas mark 7. Heat a large frying pan over a medium-high heat, season the racks of lamb and colour the fat-side one at a time. Once browned, brush a teaspoon of mustard over the fat of each one.

Scatter some of the herbs over the base of a roasting dish – lined with a double thickness of foil large enough to wrap the lamb up in once cooked. Drizzle over a little oil, place the racks fat-side up on top, then scatter over some more herbs and drizzle over a little more oil. Roast for about 30 minutes to leave them medium–rare. Wrap up to transport.

Kit Sharp knife, plate, knife and fork (optional)

Kit Sharp knife, plate, knife and fork (optional)

RARE ROAST BEEF WITH BALSAMIC PEPPERS

A joint of rare roast beef comes high on my list for a glam picnic, dressed up with roasted vegetables, you could add in a runny goat's cheese, some olives and other Mediterranean frills that will keep it in picnic-mode. When the French take such a joint on a picnic, they drizzle it with oil as a finishing touch, but the Cheat's Aioli (see page 30) is a perfect match. You may find it easiest to carve this joint before leaving the house, but do it as close to the picnic time as possible, and then wrap it up tightly in foil.

This slow-roasting method enhances the natural tenderness of the meat, sirloin makes a rarified treat, but the method makes a star of the more humble topside cut too. The peppers obviously turn it into a more complete event, but should you simply want a lovely joint of roast beef on its own, sear and then cook the meat in a large frying pan with a heatproof handle over a high heat. Roast the beef in the frying pan for 50 minutes to leave it rare.

For 6 people

Beef
extra virgin olive oil
1.3 1.4kg rolled topside or sirloin joint
1 scant teaspoon English mustard powder
sea salt and black pepper
1 heaped tablespoon wholegrain mustard

Peppers
4 red peppers, cores and seeds removed and
   cut into strips 3–4cm wide
2 red onions, peeled and cut into thin wedges
2 bay leaves
extra virgin olive oil
2 tablespoons balsamic vinegar

Preheat the oven to 130°C fan/140°C/gas mark 2. Heat about a teaspoon of oil in a large frying pan over a high heat. Using a tea strainer, dust the joint all over with the mustard powder and season it. Sear on all four sides, and the ends, until golden; it should be well-coloured as you're roasting at a fairly low temperature. Brush half the wholegrain mustard over the bottom of the joint using a pastry brush, and the rest over the top.

Arrange the peppers, onions and bay leaves in a large roasting dish, drizzle over 3 tablespoons of oil, season and nestle the beef in the centre. Roast the beef for 1 hour or until it registers approximately 45°C in the middle using a meat thermometer (for rare). Transfer it to a plate or wrap in foil to transport.

Turn the oven up to 220°C fan/230°C/gas mark 8, drizzle half the balsamic vinegar over the peppers and onions and stir, then continue to roast for 10–20 minutes until golden and syrupy. Drizzle over the remaining tablespoon of balsamic vinegar and stir. Thinly carve the beef and serve with the peppers.

Kit Sharp knife, plate, knife and fork (optional)

AUBERGINE VEGGIE ROAST WITH GOAT'S CHEESE AND TOMATOES

Roast-aubergine slices, crisp on the outside and deliciously succulent within, piled up with tomatoes and goat's cheese makes an excellent veggie picnic roast.

For 6 people

3 aubergine, sliced approx. 3cm thick, ends discarded
extra virgin olive oil
sea salt and black pepper

300g cherry tomatoes, halved or quartered, depending on size
150g young firm goat's cheese (such as Perroche), cut into approx. 1cm dice
coarsely chopped flat-leaf parsley

Preheat the oven to 200°C fan/210°C/gas mark 7. Lay the aubergine slices out on a couple of baking trays, with a little space between each slice. Brush the slices with oil on both sides and season the top. Roast for 20 minutes, then turn them and cook for another 15–20 minutes until golden. At the same time, scatter a little salt over the tomatoes in a bowl and set aside.

Transfer the aubergine slices to a large roasting dish that holds them in a single layer with a little space in between. Pour 3 tablespoons of oil over the tomatoes and gently toss, and mix in the goat's cheese. Pile this on top of the aubergine slices and return to the oven for 4–5 minutes to warm through, then leave to cool. Scatter with lots of chopped parsley. Transport in the roasting dish covered with foil, or transfer to a plate or container and cover.

Kit Serving spoon, plate, knife and fork

VITELLO TONNATO

For extra-special occasions, vitello tonnato never fails to please. Your best bet here is a joint of topside.

For 6 people

Veal
1 teaspoon extra virgin olive oil
sea salt and black pepper
900g topside of veal
1 small onion, peeled, halved and sliced
a couple of sprigs of rosemary
150ml white wine

Sauce
1 medium organic egg yolk
75g tuna fish in brine (approx. ½ x 130g tin)
4 salted anchovy fillets
250ml olive oil, or 150ml extra virgin olive oil and
    100ml groundnut oil
1 tablespoon lemon juice
approx. 4 tablespoons veal cooking liquor
a jar of capers, and of salted anchovies, to serve

Preheat the oven to 130°C fan/140°C/gas mark 2. Heat the oil in a large frying pan over a high heat. Season the veal with salt and pepper and sear on all sides until well coloured. Place the veal in a roasting dish that will hold it snugly on top of the onion and rosemary. Pour the wine into the base. Cover with foil and roast for about 1 hour or until a meat thermometer reaches 55–60°C inserted into the centre of the thickest section (for medium–rare) and it feels soft when pressed, start checking it after about 50 minutes. Transfer the veal to a plate, cover with foil and leave to cool. Slice the veal wafer thin and wrap in foil.

Strain the cooking juices and use them in the sauce. To make the sauce, whizz the egg yolk, tuna fish and anchovies to a paste in a food-processor. Slowly incorporate half the oil with the motor running as though making a mayonnaise, scraping down the sides as you go if necessary. Add the lemon juice, then incorporate the remaining oil and about 4 tablespoons of the veal cooking juice, which will be more or less all of it, you should have a rich pouring sauce. Serve the veal coated with the sauce, with some capers and an anchovy fillet on the side.

Kit Serving spoon, plate, knife and fork

GRAND SALMON

As fashions change, this dish has the same appeal as the whole poached salmon of yesteryear. A fish this size makes a big but an affordable splash, especially if you buy a good farmed salmon.

For 10 people

2 tablespoons each of finely chopped dill, chives
  and flat-leaf parsley
1 teaspoon fennel seeds, coarsely ground
sea salt and black pepper
1 x approx. 3kg salmon, cleaned and scaled,
  head and tail removed
4 tablespoons extra virgin olive oil
juice of 1 lemon
3 tablespoons white wine

Caper Mayonnaise
200g mayonnaise
a squeeze of lemon juice and ½ teaspoon finely
  grated lemon zest
2 tablespoons capers, rinsed and coarsely
  chopped

Blend all the ingredients in a bowl or container.
Chill or keep in a cool place.

Preheat the oven to 200°C fan/210°C/gas mark 7 and preheat the grill. Combine the herbs and fennel seeds with a teaspoon of salt and about the same amount of black pepper.

Score the salmon flesh diagonally on both sides at 5cm intervals with deep slits and season the fish with salt and pepper. Lay a double thickness of foil on top of your grill pan so it is a little longer than the fish. Lay the salmon on top, cupping the edges of the foil, and grill one side for 3–4 minutes until the skin blisters and colours, then stuff half of the herbs into the slits, turn and repeat with the other side.

Pour over the olive oil, lemon juice and wine and roast, uncovered, for 40–45 minutes. Check whether it is cooked by slipping a sharp knife between the backbone and the flesh. The flesh should easily lift off the bones, if it clings or looks translucent then it needs a little longer. You can fillet the fish before going, in which case leave it to cool.

Kit Sharp knife, serving spoon, plate, knife and fork

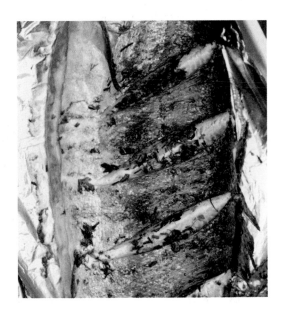

HOT FOOD ON LOCATION

Some of my fondest memories of

picnics revolve around what can at best be described as dodgy weather. Lighting fires on blustery Hebridean beaches, buttoned to the chin and shivering, huddling around a stack of smoking logs and grilling scallops or kippers in between sandcastle and dam-building duty is a parental rite of passage, and a fine lunch at the end is a great reward. Food doesn't get much better or tastier than in those kind of circumstances, so it's worth every heave of the spade.

That said, there is dodgy and there is dodgy; and a little spell – however brief – of sunshine works wonders for any occasion. Searing heatwaves, however, that leave you wishing you could stay in the car when you get there to take advantage of the air-con are by no means the best time to be packing up with a view to taking off for lunch. Not least because you will need to find shade when you arrive, there is only so much that sunblock and floppy hats can do. So, a windswept beach, an autumnal wood or meadowscape at Easter, beautiful if chilly, can make for truly lovely outdoor gatherings. The foil to this, if we want to be exceptionally civilised, is something warming along the way. And even if it isn't chilly (do we really need an excuse?), I love picnics that mix it up, some grilled food thrown in with the usual spread, and

the offer of a small cup of soup to begin is unlikely to result in rejection.

This is where small travelling barbecues come into their own. They can be preloaded with briquettes and firelighters at home, ready for lighting at the strike of a match. Cooking on a picnic may find us less well-prepared than when we are camping – that bijou kitchen-in-a-box begins to seem like a luxury when you have no water, no chopping board and no knives. So, the answer is to have absolutely everything done at home before you go. Get whatever it is you are cooking ready as far as is humanly possible in an airtight container, at the ready for grilling.

Alternatively, fast forward to a dank and drizzly day, walking in the woods kicking through damp leaves or the long wet grasses of an orchard after a spring shower. We might play this slightly differently to our summer picnics, out goes the basket and in comes a backpack or shoulder bag, and a coat is as good as a rug for sitting on. The chances are we don't want to sit around, but rest and recharge. Again, think of the pleasurable promise of a flask of steaming hot soup that can be poured into mugs to revive numbing fingers as well as doing that porridge-like thing of heating you from the inside out.

'A windswept beach, an autumnal wood or meadowscape at Easter, beautiful if chilly, can make for truly lovely outdoor gatherings.'

FOOD IN A FLASK

REAL PORRIDGE WITH WHISKY

However beautiful the morning, there will almost certainly be a nip in the air, and maybe a dew if it's a lovely summer's day. The best porridge splutters away for some 20 minutes – it's worth going to the trouble of cooking this with proper oatmeal. To be truly decadent, take a small jar of soft brown sugar, a hip flask of whisky and a small pot of cream.

For 4 people

175g medium oatmeal
1.2 litres water
½ teaspoon sea salt

light brown muscovado or demerara sugar, whisky
and double cream, to serve

Place the oatmeal, water and salt in a saucepan (ideally, a non-stick one) and bring to the boil over a high heat, stirring constantly. Reduce the heat to low and continue to cook for 25 minutes until the oatmeal is swollen and thickened, stirring occasionally.

The porridge will be thinner than you would normally make it, allowing for it to firm up in the flask. Pour it into a food flask or wide-necked vacuum flask. Give it a stir before dishing up with sugar, whisky for those that want, and plenty of cream.

Kit Long spoon for stirring, bowls or cups, spoons

ROAST TOMATO SOUP

Soups don't get any simpler than this, or tomato soups much better or more vibrant. Quite simply, it's a magical concoction of tomatoes, onions and olive oil – no stock is required, the roasting does for that as well as bringing out the flavour of the vegetables at the same time.

For 6 people

2.25kg tomatoes, left on the vine
3 red onions, peeled, and cut into wedges
extra virgin olive oil
sea salt and black pepper
celery salt
1½ teaspoons caster sugar

Preheat the oven to 220°C fan/230°C/gas mark 8. Arrange the tomatoes and onions in a couple of large roasting dishes in a single layer, drizzle over 5 tablespoons of oil and roast for 20 minutes. Allow to cool.

Once they are cool enough to handle, pinch the tomatoes off the vines using a fork, and tip into a liquidiser with the onions and roasting juices. Add a good dose of salt, some celery salt, some black pepper, the sugar, and another 5 tablespoons of oil and liquidise. Pass through a sieve into a saucepan and gently reheat before pouring into a vacuum flask.

Kit Cups or bowls, spoons

SPICY BUTTERNUT SQUASH SOUP

Have some fun here and experiment with squashes and pumpkins you might not normally buy. Butternut squash promises to be the sweetest of all, but you can always add a little sugar if you feel the call is there.

For 6 people

50g unsalted butter
1 large onion, peeled and chopped
2 tablespoons chopped fresh ginger
2 x 900g butternut squash, skinned,
  deseeded and coarsely chopped
1 litre fresh vegetable or chicken stock
sea salt and black pepper
150g crème fraîche
freshly grated nutmeg

Melt the butter in a large saucepan over a medium heat, add the onion, ginger and squash and fry for about 5 minutes, stirring frequently, until glossy. Add the stock and plenty of seasoning, pressing the squash down to submerge it, bring to the boil and simmer for 10–15 minutes or until the squash is tender. Liquidise the soup in batches in a blender with the crème fraiche and a generous grating of nutmeg, then pass it through a sieve. Gently reheat before transferring to a vacuum flask.

Kit Cups or bowls, spoons

FRENCH ONION SOUP

The earthy and gutsy character of French onion soup makes it ideal cockle-warming stuff. It's that slug of brandy at the end, which requires a hip flask of the liquor, which will, of course, need finishing off before you return in order to lighten the load, making for a merry time on a chilly day. Large paper cups or bowls are ideal here, as you can put the grated cheese into the base and stack them before you leave, at the ready to receive the hot soup from a flask, no washing up to follow.

For 4 people

50g unsalted butter
3 onions, peeled, halved and thinly sliced
150ml white wine
900ml chicken stock
sea salt and black pepper
75g grated Gruyère
2 tablespoons brandy (optional)
crusty bread, to serve

Melt the butter in a large saucepan over a medium heat and fry the onions for 20-30 minutes until a deep even gold, stirring frequently. It's really important to take your time here and not rush. Add the wine and simmer until well reduced, then add the chicken stock and some seasoning, bring to the boil and simmer over a low heat for 10 minutes. The soup can be made in advance, in which case reheat and pour boiling hot into a wide-necked food flask.

Divide the Gruyère between four cups (you can do this before leaving home if you like). Pour the hot soup over and add a little brandy, if wished. Serve with bread.

Kit Cups or bowls, spoons

MEATBALL AND BEAN CASSEROLE

A really rustic soup, the sausage plays the role of meatballs which get wolfed down, and there are enough cans involved to ensure it isn't too arduous.

For 6 people

1–2 tablespoons extra virgin olive oil
8 chipolatas, skinned and thickly sliced
125g chorizo sausages, raw or cooked, halved
  and sliced 1cm thick
2 onions, peeled and chopped
1 celery heart, trimmed and sliced
½ small Savoy cabbage, finely sliced and cut
  into 4–5cm lengths
150ml white wine

1 x 400g can chopped tomatoes
1 x 400g can chickpeas, drained and rinsed
1 x 400g can flageolet or haricot beans, drained
  and rinsed
1 litre chicken stock
sea salt
a pinch of chilli flakes
2 large handfuls of coarsely chopped flat-leaf
  parsley, plus extra to serve

Heat a tablespoon of oil in a large saucepan over a medium heat and fry the sausage and chorizo for 5–10 minutes until lightly coloured, carefully turning them with a spatula now and again, then transfer them to a bowl.

If necessary add another tablespoon of oil to the pan, but there should be plenty given out by the sausages, and fry the onion and celery for 10–15 minutes until golden and glossy, stirring occasionally. Add the cabbage and cook for several minutes until wilted, then add the wine and tomatoes and simmer to reduce by half. Return the sausages to the pan, add the chickpeas and beans, the stock, plenty of salt and the chilli. Bring to the boil and simmer for 10 minutes.

Taste for seasoning and stir in the parsley, although you could also take this separately to add just before eating, if wished. Transfer to a food flask.

Kit Cups or bowls, spoons

GRILLS

Nothing that follows by way of grills, I promise, is going to take you more than 10 minutes before the off. One of the pluses of having a barbecue on location, has to be that you can call on it when you don't have time even for the usual half hour or so in the kitchen to rustle up some salads or sarnies. These grills are designed to be 'shop and go'.

My favourite travel barbecue hasn't changed since we wrote *The Camping Cookbook*, the bijoux Weber Smokey Joe gets my vote every time, not least because it comes with a lid (see page 16); although if you are grilling without a lid, then it is worth keeping a water spray to hand to quell any flare-ups.

Beyond this, Top Tip number 1 has to be to remember to get your coals really hot before you start grilling. The timings given on a packet of briquettes have a habit of looking on the bright side, if it says they heat up in 20 minutes, you can count on a good hour before they will be covered in that desirable fine layer of white ash that's so important to good results. And here especially, where the foods are all fast-cooking by design, that heat is all-important.

Top Tip number 2, is to throw away that half bag of briquettes from last summer, if it happens to be the first barbecue of the season. If it's been sitting in a shed or garage there is every chance they will be damp and never get properly hot. I hope that by putting this in writing that I will actually start to follow my own advice on this one. I habitually forget over the winter.

Weber Smokey Joe

'By having a barbecue on location, you can call on it when you don't have time for the half hour in the kitchen to rustle up some salads or sarnies.'

TRAVELLER'S CROQUE MONSIEUR

Travelling around France in search of a decent Croque Monsieur becomes an increasingly dispiriting business. In fact, it is hard to believe that such a simple creation can have become so warped by the need for convenience. The fact we search at all is that there is no toasted sandwich to beat it – there is something magical about that crisp toasted cushion oozing nutty Gruyère laced with Dijon mustard, and a thick slice of roast ham – you are guaranteed the finest results if you make them yourself. The good news is that they can be assembled well in advance, and they travel.

For 2 people

unsalted butter, softened for spreading
4 x 1cm slices of coarse-textured white bread,
    such as pain de Campagne
200g Gruyère, thinly sliced
2–4 slices of honey-roast ham
Dijon mustard

AT HOME
Butter the bread on both sides. Cover two of the slices with a layer of Gruyère, then a layer of ham, smear over some mustard and cover with another layer of Gruyère. Close the sandwiches with the top layers of bread. They can be prepared to this point in advance, in which case, wrap in clingfilm and chill until you're ready to go.

ON LOCATION
Toast the sandwiches on the outside of the grill, turning them round now and again so they toast evenly, for 2–4 minutes either side or until golden and crisp and the cheese within has melted. Cut the toasted sandwiches in half for eating with napkins.

Kit Barbecue (preloaded with briquettes, firelighters, matches), spatula, sharp knife, serving plate, napkins

SAUSAGE SPLITS

Could this be the answer to avoiding burnt sausages? By slitting them open, you halve the thickness of the sausage, cutting down on the time needed to grill them. And the insides cook to that especially alluring caramelised finish usually found in the bits that burst out from a sausage as it cooks.

For 6 people

6 pork sausages (1 x 450g pack)
6 finger rolls
3 tablespoons soured cream
3 tablespoons mayonnaise

2 teaspoons Dijon mustard
baby leaves and cocktail gherkins, rinsed and
   halved lengthways, to serve

AT HOME
Slit the sausages lengthways and open them out so they are evenly thick. Slit the rolls open, leaving them attached at the side. Blend the soured cream, mayonnaise and mustard in a sealable bowl or container. Wrap the sausages and rolls in foil.

ON LOCATION
Barbecue the sausages for 4–5 minutes each side, skin-side down first, which will set the cut surface on top. Briefly toast the buns on either side. Place a sausage in each open bun, pile with some leaves, drizzle over the sauce and adorn with a few cocktail gherkins.

Kit Barbecue (preloaded with briquettes, firelighters, matches), tongs

BASIL BURGERS

I once managed to horrify a family member, who was kindly babysitting, by suggesting that she made the children some hamburgers for supper. 'Ground meat, chopped shallot, salt and pepper and shape into a disc,' I explained, to assuage her appalled expression. 'Well I doubt I'll go to the trouble of chopping a shallot,' she replied. But yes, it really is that simple, even if I have taken the liberty of adding a little basil here and some sumac – the ground rust-red berries that have traditionally replaced lemon in the mountainous regions of Lebanon. You can also make delicious kofta burgers. Simply combine the lamb with 25g each of finely chopped **coriander** and **flat-leaf parsley** (leaves and fine stalks), 1 small peeled and finely chopped **onion**, ¼ teaspoon **cayenne**, a teaspoon of **cumin** and of **sea salt**.

For 4 people/Makes 8 mini-burgers

50g basil leaves
2 shallots, peeled
1 teaspoon sumac
1 garlic clove, peeled
sea salt and black pepper
extra virgin olive oil
600g minced lamb
pitta breads, hummus and coriander sprigs,
   to serve

AT HOME

Place all the ingredients for the burgers except for the lamb in a food-processor with 1 tablespoon of oil and reduce to a coarse purée. Blend this with the lamb in a large bowl and form into eight burgers, by shaping balls of the mixture the size of a clementine. These can be made in advance, if so cover and chill them.

ON LOCATION

Grill the burgers over a hot barbecue for a few minutes either side until golden brown and firm when pressed. They find a natural home in a warm pitta pocket with a dollop of hummus and a few coriander leaves.

Kit Barbecue (preloaded with briquettes, firelighters, matches), tongs, sharp knife

LEMON CHICKEN FILLETS WITH CRISPY BACON

Chicken marinated with lemon and eaten with a slice of crispy bacon makes a fab picnic line-up. The temptation to add in some flat-leaf parsley (something my husband says I use far too much of) is almost too hard to resist, but over to you on that one. Just a little at the end perhaps. I would serve them slipped inside pitta breads or with a green or tomato salad.

For 4 people

4 skinless chicken fillets (approx. 500–600g)
finely grated zest and juice of 1 lemon
5 tablespoons extra virgin olive oil
sea salt and black pepper

4 rashers of unsmoked rindless streaky bacon
coarsely chopped flat-leaf parsley, to serve
(optional)

AT HOME
Cut out the white tendon on the underside of the chicken fillets, if visible. Whisk the lemon zest, juice and olive oil in an airtight sealable container. Add the chicken fillets, toss to coat, then put on the lid.

ON LOCATION
Season the chicken and barbecue for 5–7 minutes on either side until golden and firm when pressed. Barbecue the bacon on both sides for 3–4 minutes in total (if there is room on the barbecue, this can be done at the same time as the chicken).

Drizzle a little of the marinade over the chicken, top with a sliver of bacon, and scatter over some parsley, if wished.

Kit Barbecue (preloaded with briquettes, firelighters, matches), tongs, sharp knife

JEAN-CHRISTOPHE'S CHICKEN WINGS

The reputation of these chicken wings follows in the wake of their creator Jean-Christophe Chavaillard, a larger-than-life Norman restauranteur whose former domaine Equinoxe, suggests the spirit within – a bar on one side frequented by salty old sea-dogs, and women in faded Lanvin scarves inevitably accompanied by a 'monsieur d'un certain age' filling the tables of the dining salon. Moules and huîtres floated between the two bridging the cultural divide and everyone got along famously. Sadly, such was his success that he then moved to a bigger, better bar and dining salon overlooking the Baie du Mont Saint Michel. I had the good fortune to acquire the secret of his sticky chicken wings before he left.

Makes 12

Marinade
4 tablespoons extra virgin olive oil
1 tablespoon finely chopped rosemary
1 tablespoon finely chopped thyme
2 bay leaves, torn into pieces
3 garlic cloves, peeled and crushed to a paste
Chicken
12 chicken wings
1 tablespoon Dijon mustard
1 tablespoon runny honey
sea salt and black pepper

AT HOME
Combine all the ingredients for the marinade in a large bowl. Add the chicken wings and coat them, then cover and chill overnight.

Blend the mustard and honey in a small bowl. Turn the wings in their marinade and season.

ON LOCATION
Barbecue the wings for 10–20 minutes until they seem half cooked and mid-gold, turning them once and moving them around as necessary, then brush on both sides with the mustard-honey glaze and cook for approximately 10 minutes more, again turning them once, until golden.

Kit Barbecue (preloaded with briquettes, firelighters, matches), tongs

MINTY LAMB CHOPS WITH COURGETTES

If you can't quite leave Sunday roast lamb with mint sauce behind, then give this outdoor take on it a whirl. Courgettes always grill up a treat, turning gorgeously sweet in the throes of cooking, which takes care of meat and one veg. Some ripe tomatoes would, as ever, be lovely here too.

For 4 people

2 teaspoons mint sauce
a squeeze of lemon juice
sea salt and black pepper
6 tablespoons extra virgin olive oil

300g courgettes, ends discarded and sliced
    lengthways
6 x 800g lamb chops, 2–3cm thick

AT HOME
Whisk the mint sauce, lemon juice and a little salt with 4 tablespoons of olive oil in a small sealed container until amalgamated. Put the courgette slices in a sealable container with the remaining olive oil and some seasoning. Put the lid on the container and turn it a few times to coat the courgettes.

ON LOCATION
Season the lamb chops and barbecue for 3–4 minutes each side until golden and firm, but with a slight give when pressed. Transfer to a plate and cover with foil, if you have some. Barbecue the courgette slices for a few minutes on each side, the first side may take a little longer. Serve the chops and courgette slices with the mint dressing spooned over.

Kit Barbecue (preloaded with briquettes, firelighters, matches), plate, foil, knife and fork (optional)

STEAK WITH GARLIC BUTTER

A whizzy garlic butter with watercress sets off the steak beautifully and makes for fab sandwiches (pop on top of a slice of grilled sourdough drizzled with olive oil). Or, serve the steak French auberge style with a packet of skinny potato chips.

For 4 people

4 x 150g sirloin or rump steaks, beaten
   1–2 cm thick
30g Boursin
30g salted butter, softened
extra virgin olive oil
sea salt and black pepper
watercress or rocket, to serve

AT HOME
If necessary beat the steaks to the right thickness. Blend the Boursin and butter in a small container.

ON LOCATION
Drizzle a little olive oil either side of the steaks, then season. Barbecue for 2 minutes on one side for medium–rare, or 3 minutes for medium. (If cooking on a kettle or closed barbecue, leave the lid off and use a spatula to press down on the steak, which will enhance the stripes.) Turn the steaks, roughly spread with the garlic butter, then barbecue for another 2–3 minutes, again uncovered, until they feel firm but have a slight give, by which time the garlic butter should be well on its way to being melted. Carefully transfer the steaks to a plate and leave to rest for 5 minutes. Serve with a pile of watercress or rocket.

Kit Barbecue (preloaded with briquettes, firelighters, matches), spatula, plate, knife and fork (optional)

FONDUE MUSHROOM BURGERS

This luxurious veggie take on the burger option also works well as a side dish with grilled chicken, lamb or pork.

For 4 people

8 Portobello mushrooms, stalks trimmed level with cups
150g Comté or Gruyère, thinly sliced
thickly sliced pickled chillies (such as Fragata Guindillas)
extra virgin olive oil
sea salt and black pepper
80g (approx. 3 tablespoons) crème fraîche
4 pitta breads, to serve

AT HOME
Trim the mushrooms and slice the cheese and pickled chillies.

ON LOCATION
Drizzle some of the olive oil over either side of the mushrooms, then season. Barbecue, cupped-side down, for 10 minutes, then turn them, fill the cavities with slivers of cheese and a heaped teaspoon of crème fraîche and grill for another 10 minutes.

Briefly warm the pittas either side on the barbecue. Halve and open out the pockets. Pop a mushroom inside each one with some sliced pickled chilli.

Kit Barbecue (preloaded with briquettes, firelighters, matches), spatula

POOLSIDE PRAWNS

Poolside, seaside, riverside, almost any picnic that involves nearby water has the added allure of swimming thrown in. As a child there was a large open air 1930s swimming pool close to where we lived, unheated, which meant that on the average beautiful Sunday morning we had it all to ourselves. My father used to take my brothers and I there on a regular basis for a swim followed by a breakfast picnic of pink-iced-sugar buns and tea on the lawn that sloped down to it. My adult taste might have migrated to the savoury scent of prawn shells toasting over hot coals, but the experience is one and the same. It is the shell that encapsulates that bisque-like scent, which infuses the prawns within. There is no need to think further than a sachet of salt in which to dip them as they are peeled. And if you do happen to be on a beach, if you are after the perfect chain of events, then stroll down to the water to wash your fingers, taking some really ripe mangoes or peaches, and lie in the shallows to eat them.

For 4–6 people

500g unshelled tiger prawns or langoustines
sea salt
Marinade
1 teaspoon fennel seeds
1 tablespoon lemon juice
2 tablespoons extra virgin olive oil
1 teaspoon finely chopped medium-hot red chilli

AT HOME

Grind the fennel seeds in a pestle and mortar, then combine with the rest of the ingredients for the marinade in an airtight container. Add the prawns, close and give it a few shakes to coat them, then chill until leaving.

ON LOCATION

Just before grilling, season the prawns with salt, close the container and turn it a few times. Barbecue for 1–2 minutes each side until pink and firm when pressed. Eat with your fingers as an appetiser with drinks.

Kit Barbecue (preloaded with briquettes, firelighters, matches), tongs

HOTDOGS FROM HEAVEN

Sausages provide one of the great no-hassle solutions to entertaining any number of people, and they are international; pretty much every country has its own take on sausages. The ideal here is to grill up lots of different types, juicy free-range pork bangers, venison or wild boar, Bratwurst and Frankfurters, Toulouse sausages, Merguez and the like. Then, dish them up with a pile of bread and a few relishes and you have some serious hotdog heaven.

Vegetarians needn't dispair. See if you can find some Glamorgan sausages made with Caerphilly or Lancashire cheese, or grill up some of the Fondue Mushroom Burgers (see page 139).
You can fit a fair number of sausages on a portable grill, enough for 6–8 people, and they cook sufficiently quickly that you should be able to fit several batches in while the coals are hot, within the space of about an hour.

Finger or torpedo rolls are an obvious vehicle, but markets in France that set you the challenge of going inside without succumbing to the lure of the foot-long meaty sausages grilling at the entrance, invariably take it no further than a length of baguette, finished with a squeeze of ketchup and of mustard. And they are quite the best hotdogs around.

All the following recipes serve 6–8 people

1.2kg sausages – a selection of any you like: Cumberland, Toulouse, free-range pork, venison, wild boar, Merguez, Frankfurters

Without pricking the sausages, lay them on the barbecue rack spaced about 1cm apart to ensure they caramelise evenly. The exact time it will take for each type of sausage to cook will depend, about 20–30 minutes in total. Tend them assiduously, they can easily colour and burn, so move any that are cooking quickly to the outside. Remove the sausages as they are cooked and keep them warm, covered with foil, if you have some.

BREADS

Pile 'em high – in a wicker tray lined with a linen napkin or tea-towel, or a big bamboo plate. My favourites for hotdogs are baguettes, pitta breads and soft torpedo-shaped rolls.

ROASTED RED ONIONS

Heat the oven to 170°C fan/180°C/gas mark 5. Lay 900g peeled, halved and sliced **red onions** in a thin layer on two baking sheets, breaking the slices into rings as far as possible. Drizzle over a little **extra virgin olive oil** and roast for 35 minutes, stirring halfway through to ensure they caramelise evenly. Place them in a bowl and toss with a teaspoon of **red wine vinegar** and some **sea salt** and **black pepper**. Wrap in foil to transport, rewarming the package for a few minutes on either side on the barbecue to freshen them.

MUSTARD SAUCE

Whisk together 300g **soured cream**, 4 heaped teaspoons **Dijon mustard**, a few drops of **lemon juice** and **sea salt**.

HOTDOG ESSENTIALS

Take some **Oven-baked Sweet Tomato and Chilli Relish** (see page 58; this oven-baked version is speedier than most recipes) and **tomato ketchup**. I wouldn't even think of making your own; the assembled company will only silently remonstrate that it's not the real thing, and it does at least come in plastic bottles. Some **salad leaves**, such as **rocket or watercress**, pack a nice punch to counterbalance all that meatiness.

Kit Barbecue (preloaded with briquettes, firelighters, matches), tongs, knife, spoon (for chilli jam)

'Dish up the sausages with a pile of bread and a few relishes and you have some serious hotdog heaven.'

A HAPPY ENDING

The most relaxing picnics are a

slow but steady transition from vertical to sitting, to lying gazing up at a canopy of leaves with something sweet in hand. However rough the affair, that small but sugary ending provides a note of civilisation, a reminder of a progression of courses that we might anticipate in a restaurant or as a part of dinner at home. So, this is a big chapter, not least because so many picnics take in tea as well as pud, so we need lots of ideas for biscuits and cakes as well as easy finales.

Not that you have to get baking, plenty of treats come ready for the off, such as a chilled bar of chocolate, one of those large Desperate Dan ones should silence any juniors. While my own idea of no-cook heaven is a punnet of locally grown strawberries or blueberries purchased on the morning from the market. But I also can't quite resist a little cooking on site, well perhaps cooking is too grand a word for the sort of mashing and stirring to a mess that I had in mind. There are all manner of yummy creations that can be whisked up from a bag of meringues, some berries and a tub of crème fraîche, clotted cream or mascarpone, the essentials for a rustic Eton Mess. Or forego all that and pass the ingredients

separately – by way of a deconstructed pud that can be assembled on a plate for handing round once you are there.

Beyond this, all sorts of cakes and biscuits can play a part. Anything that comes in a paper case is ideal, we can live without cupcakes and all that icing, but little chocolate crispies are ideal, or flapjacks – ever my default last-minute solution. The salt caramel ones (see page 158) are wolfed down in our house. Traybakes are also brilliant – take them in their tin and it doubles as a serving plate, and they spread to any number of people. Springform cake tins too provide a means of transporting and protecting a cake, until you get there when the collar is easily slipped off and the base again stands in as a plate. Loaf cakes are also pretty friendly, in which case wrap them in foil or clingfilm and slice them to order. Plain as it is, a Madeira can be married with any seasonal fruit, and offers an excuse to slip a half bottle of sweet wine into the coldbag.

And just occasionally, when the call is for a 'proper' pud as such, something to tackle with a spoon, I would either opt for a colourful jelly made in silicone muffin moulds, or more decadently make a tiramisu in a large clip-topped jar.

'My own idea of no-cook heaven is a punnet of locally grown strawberries or blueberries purchased on the morning from the market.'

LET'S GO: FINALES

A BAR OF CHOCOLATE

If you plan on nothing else for pudding, then a bar of chocolate (or several) is a must. If it is a mega bar, then a spell in the fridge before you leave, is a good idea. And if it is a thin bar or bars, then I would pop it into the freezer to preserve that crisp bite. Frozen chocolate always brings back memories of leaving a bar of Milka on the balcony on skiing holidays in Austria as a child – by far the high point of the trip.

TURKISH DELIGHT

You want the real thing here, generous jellied cubes headily scented with rosewater and liberally dusted with icing sugar.

BAKLAVA

Anything involving honey is risky on a picnic and likely to cause more pain than pleasure once it starts to attract unwanted winged friends, but a little **baklava** stashed in a white cardboard box will see to the craving for something sticky to go with any fruit.

MACARONS

Very Marie Antoinette, and as we know what was good enough for her… The buttercream in these does render them on the fragile side, but a patisserie box full of pastel-hued **macarons** completes any line-up of summer fruit – **cherries**, **strawberries**, **raspberries**, **figs**, **plums** and **peaches**.

DATES WITH GORGONZOLA

Slit fudgey **Medjool dates** and fill with a gooey **Gorgonzola dolce**.

WATERMELON WITH FETA

Hack a small **watermelon**, preferably unseeded, into crescents and dish up with a slab of **feta**. You could build on this combination with **green olives** and **Parma ham**, too, and offer it up as an amuse bouche.

PEARS WITH PARMESAN

Any juicy ripe **pears** will do here, **Comice or Conference**, that go hand in glove with a crumbly aged **Parmesan** that's been hacked into nibs.

FIGS WITH GOAT'S CHEESE

The faint sourness of a young **goat's cheese** and a touch of salt bring out the fragrance of ripe **figs**.

MANCHEGO WITH QUINCE CHEESE

A sliver of grainy **Spanish Manchego** with an even finer sliver of perfumed **membrillo** is a classic. Throw in some crisp **roasted almonds** to share in the cultural heritage.

APPLES WITH CHEDDAR

We're so spoilt for choice of fruits today, that munching on an apple can seem banal. But the finer **apple** varieties eaten with a **farmhouse Cheddar** makes for rarefied grazing, and a picnic allows us the time and space to savour them. A **mature Gouda** also marries beautifully with slivers of apple; throw in some **walnuts** and you'll have a light meal. In fact, you can wheel this one out as a big splash with different varieties of apple and a couple of cheeses (**Cantal** is another good one), and in the late summer or early autumn sunshine include a bottle of **Calvados** or other fiery spirit.

IN A MESS

SUN-BAKED BANANAS

I am not the first to try to harness the heat given off by engines and automobiles as a secondary source of energy. My late father-in-law Tony Bell, who was drafted into Caen just after D-Day, enjoyed fine lunches of chicken roasted on the exhaust box of his Churchill tank as they slowly made their progression to Arnhem and then the Black Forest. It's unlikely that you're picnicking in a tank, but should you have driven to the location on a hot day (say 23°C or above), point the bonnet into the full sun and turn that negative 'too hot to pack any chocolate', into a positive.

Before leaving home, individually wrap unpeeled **bananas** in foil, and transport a bar of **dark or milk chocolate**. On arriving at your destination, open up the package, slit the banana and pop a row of chocolate down the centre, then position the bananas with the foil open on the dashboard and leave them for 30–60 minutes until the chocolate has melted. A tub of **crème fraîche** in the coldbag and pudding's complete.

BANANA FOOL

Pack a tub of **crème fraîche** in the coldbag, and take some **bananas** and a small sachet of **soft brown sugar**. Slice the bananas into a large bowl, add about a third of the amount of crème fraîche and combine, then sprinkle over some sugar.

STRAWBERRY CREAMS

Gariguette strawberries and their ilk, or wild ones, are heart-stoppingly tender. They have only a day's shelf-life once ripe if you are lucky – they collapse at the touch of a fork or spoon – which makes them perfect for a heady whisked-up summer cream. Otherwise, ensure your berries are ripe to the point of melting, and leave them in the sun once you arrive to soften them further.

Pack a tub of **mascarpone** in the coldbag, and take a punnet of very ripe small **strawberries**, you want equal quantities of both. Hull and mash half of these with the mascarpone using a spoon or fork in a large bowl, adding **icing or vanilla sugar** to taste, then fold through the remainder, and scoop up with **dessert biscuits**.

ETON MESS

Take a bag of **meringues**, a punnet of **raspberries** and a tub of **crème fraîche**. Come pud, layer these in a large bowl, starting with crushed meringues, then cream and then fruit. Repeat this depending on how many mouths there are to feed.

STRAWBERRY SHORTCAKE

Take a punnet of **strawberries** and leave these to warm in the sun on your arrival, and pack a tub of **crème fraîche** in the coldbag, and also take some good **shortbread**. Arrange these together on a large plate for everyone to assemble their own strawberry shortcake.

PEACH MELBA ON A PLATE

Pack some ripe **peaches** and **raspberries** and leave these to warm in the sun on your arrival. Pop a tub of **mascarpone** in the coldbag and arrange halved peaches with the raspberries and the mascarpone on a large plate for handing round.

TRIFLE ON A PLATE

Pack up a bag of **amaretti** and some ripe **apricots**, which have a particular affinity with these almond-scented biscuits, and leave the fruit to warm in the sun on arrival. Also pack a tub of **mascarpone** in the coldbag. Serve the fruits, halved and stoned, with a pile of amaretti and the tub of mascarpone to dip into on a large plate.

ALL-AMERICAN CHERRY PIE

It's the cartoon glamour of a cherry pie that is the attraction, an icon of wholesome American living, loaded with feel-good factor and comfort. Produce a homemade cherry pie and a pile of enamel plates at the end of your picnic and you can pretty much get away with buying in whatever comes before it. This pie is quite sturdy and picnic-friendly, and the way the pastry settles over the cherries looks like a sugary moonscape.

For 6 people

Sweet shortcrust pastry
200g unsalted butter, softened
150g golden caster sugar, plus extra for dusting
2 medium eggs
400g plain flour, sifted
50g ground almonds
milk, for brushing

Cherries
600g cherries, pitted
a generous squeeze of lemon juice
75g light muscovado sugar
1 tablespoon plain flour

Creaming the butter and sugar for the pastry together in the bowl of a food-processor or mixer will make light work of this. Add the eggs, then gradually add the flour and ground almonds and bring the dough together. Wrap it in clingfilm, pat into a flattened block and chill for at least 2 hours – it will keep for several days.

Preheat the oven to 180°C fan/190°C/gas mark 6. Allow the dough to come to room temperature for 15–30 minutes, and then knead it until pliable. On a lightly floured surface, thinly roll out two thirds of the dough. Use this to line the base and sides of a 23cm tart tin 3cm deep. Don't worry if the dough tears and you end up partly pressing it into the dish. Trim the sides.

Toss the cherries with the lemon juice, brown sugar and the flour, and tip them into the tart tin, spreading them out evenly. Roll out the remaining pastry, incorporating any spare trimmings, paint the pastry rim in the tin with milk and lay it over the top. Press the pastry edges together and trim the sides, then crimp the edge using the tip of your finger or else the tip of a knife. Cut a couple of small slits in the centre. Brush the surface of the pastry with milk and dust with caster sugar. Bake the pie for 30–35 minutes until the pastry is golden and the cherries are tender. Transport in the tart tin, loosely covered with foil.

Kit Pie server or sharp knife, plate, fork

ORCHARD SHORTCAKE PIE

This deep fluffy blackberry and apple pie is as much about the crumbly layers of shortcake as the fruit filling. You can serve this as a cake as well as a pud.

For 8 people

Pastry
225g self-raising flour, sifted
110g golden caster sugar
110g icing sugar, sifted
225g unsalted butter, diced
5 medium egg yolks
1 teaspoon vanilla extract
1 egg yolk blended with 1 teaspoon water
Filling
400g eating apples, peeled, quartered, cored and sliced
200g blackberries
30g golden caster sugar

Place the flour, the two sugars and butter in the bowl of a food-processor and whizz until the mixture is crumb-like. Blend the egg yolks with the vanilla in a bowl, then add to the dry ingredients and pulse to a soft, sticky dough. Wrap this in clingfilm and chill for an hour.

Preheat the oven to 170°C fan/180°C/gas mark 5, and grease a 20cm cake tin at least 7cm deep with a removeable base. Press half the dough into the tin, laying a sheet of clingfilm over the top and smoothing it with your fingers.

Toss the apples and blackberries in a bowl with the sugar and scatter over the base.

Roll out the remainder of the dough on a well-floured work surface (it will still be quite sticky) into a circle fractionally larger than the cake tin. Lay this on top of the fruit and press it into place, tidying the edges using your fingers. Liberally paint the surface with the eggwash and bake for 1 hour until deeply golden, crusty and risen. Run a knife around the collar and leave to cool, then transport in the tin, loosely covered in foil.

Kit Pie server or sharp knife, plate

ALMOND MADEIRA

I cannot be the only person in the world who adores a simple, lightly scented cake that subtly tastes of the sum of its parts – butter, sugar, eggs and, in this case, almonds. But the fashion for heavily iced buns has all but done away with this genre. At a picnic there is a real call for such a cake, with no risk of it letting the side down and melting or smothering everything in contact with sticky goo. It also works as a basic for any number of 'on site puds' as well. Team it with fragrant raspberries or strawberries and a dollop of clotted cream for an elegant pud, or eat it with crisp squares of dark chocolate and some juicy cherries.

Makes 1 x 22cm/1.3-litre loaf

180g unsalted butter, softened and diced, plus
   extra for greasing
180g golden caster sugar
4 medium eggs, separated
½ teaspoon almond or vanilla extract

125g ground almonds
125g plain flour, sifted
2 teaspoons baking powder, sifted
30g flaked almonds
icing sugar, for dusting

Preheat the oven to 170°C fan/180°C/gas mark 5 and grease a 22cm/1.3-litre non-stick loaf tin. Cream the butter and sugar together in a food-processor, then incorporate the egg yolks and the almond extract. Work in the ground almonds, flour and baking powder, then transfer the mixture to a large bowl. Whisk the egg whites in another large bowl until stiff, then fold into the cake mixture in three goes.

Transfer the mixture to the cake tin, smoothing the surface. Scatter over the almonds and bake for 55–60 minutes until golden and firm when pressed, and shrinking from the sides. Run a knife around the edge of the cake, leave it to cool and then liberally dust with icing sugar. It should keep well for several days in an airtight container.

Kit Sharp knife, plate, fork

FINANCIERS

It took me a long time to embrace silicone baking moulds, until I realised they were the answer to turning out perfect financiers, and pretty much any shape that takes your fancy will do here. If you are making them in a non-stick fairy cake tin then be sure to grease it well and run a knife around the edge of the cakes as soon as they come out of the oven.

The batter for these needs to be made ideally the night before, which fits in perfectly with most preparations. They are accommodating little sponges that can be studded with a nib of any fruit or berry, or chocolate chips, should you fancy.

Makes approx. 24

160g icing sugar, sifted
60g ground almonds
150g egg whites (4–5 medium eggs)
1 tablespoon runny honey
90g unsalted butter, melted and cooled
½ teaspoon vanilla extract

70g flour, sifted
½ teaspoon baking powder, sifted
raspberries, blueberries, 1cm nibs of peeled
    apple or apricot, dark chocolate chips,
    to decorate

Combine the icing sugar and ground almonds in a large bowl, add the egg whites and whisk to blend, then add the honey, butter and vanilla, then the flour and baking powder. Cover and chill for at least half a day, but ideally overnight.

Preheat the oven to 200°C fan/210°C/gas mark 7. If using fairy-cake moulds, then butter well, there is no need if using silicone moulds. Fill three quarters full, then decorate with one or two berries (placing raspberries hole down) or nibs of fruit, depending on the size of mould, or if making chocolate ones scatter a few chips over the top. Bake for 15–20 minutes until golden and firm. Run a knife around fairy cake moulds straight away, then leave for 5–10 minutes before removing from the tin, or popping out of the silicone moulds. Transport in an airtight container or tin, or in a pretty bag.

TRIPLE CHOCOLATE CRISPIES

One of our best-loved easy treats, these choc crispies are great if there is a posse of children to please. They come with three chocolate appeal; halfway between dark and milk, with white choc chips thrown in. It's worth making these with a high end chocolate too, the difference will show.

Makes approx. 14

100g milk chocolate, broken into pieces
100g dark chocolate (approx. 70 per cent cocoa solids), broken into pieces
25g unsalted butter
125g Rice Krispies
25g white chocolate chips

Gently melt the milk and dark chocolate with the butter in a large bowl set over a pan with a little simmering water in it, then stir in the Rice Krispies. Arrange about 14 paper cases within a couple of fairy cake tins and fill with heaped tablespoons of the mixture. Scatter a few chocolate chips over each one, chill for 30–60 minutes to set, and then store in an airtight container to transport.

SALT CARAMEL FLAPJACKS

Variation on a theme of everyone's favourite – the flapjack. These naturally lend themselves to the charm of salt caramel, with salted butter and dulce de leche (or Nestlé's Caramel Carnation) in lieu of golden syrup. It takes about as long to whisk these up as to make a cup of tea, in fact, I usually don't bother with the chocolate drizzle, but it's a nice finishing touch.

Makes 25 squares

240g lightly salted butter, diced
180g light muscovado sugar
225g dulce de leche (or Nestlé's Caramel Carnation)
350g refined rolled oats (not wholegrain)
50g dark chocolate (approx. 50 per cent cocoa solids), broken into pieces

Preheat the oven to 160°C fan/170°C/gas mark 4. Gently melt the butter with the sugar and caramel in a medium saucepan over a medium heat and whisk until smooth and amalgamated. Stir in the oats, tip the mixture into a 23cm square brownie tin or equivalent in size, pressing it down using the back of a metal spoon, and bake for 20 minutes until very lightly coloured.

Leave to cool for about 30 minutes, then gently melt the chocolate in a bowl set over a pan of simmering water, and drizzle this over the flapjack. Set aside for several hours for the chocolate to set, then cut into 25 squares. Wrap in foil or stack in a tin to transport.

FARMHOUSE SULTANA CAKE

Sultanas are the most succulent and sweet of all dried grapes, and this lightly fruited cake has hearty outdoor spirit without being overly heavy. Wheel it out at teatime on an all-day picnic, once you've exhausted the cricket or dam-building on the beach and hunger is starting to bite. It's also just the ticket with a sip of port or sherry on a crisp autumnal morning before going off on a ramble. And like most fruit cakes, it finds a natural friend in a sliver of Cheddar or other hard cheese.

Makes 1 x 20cm cake

170g plain flour
170g ground almonds
3 teaspoons baking powder
1 heaped teaspoon mixed spice
150g light muscovado sugar
150g unsalted butter, diced

4 medium eggs
50ml milk
325g sultanas
75g mixed peel
dark rum, for brushing
caster sugar, for dusting

Preheat the oven to 150°C fan/160°C/gas mark 3. Place the flour, ground almonds, baking powder, spice and sugar in the bowl of a food-processor, add the butter and whizz to a fine crumble. Now add the eggs, and then the milk. Transfer the mixture to a large bowl and fold in the sultanas and the mixed peel.

Grease and line with baking paper both the base and the sides of a 20cm cake tin 7cm deep – you can use a dab of the cake mixture to glue the side ends in place. Spoon the mixture into the prepared tin, mounding it in the centre, and bake for about 75 minutes or until a skewer inserted into the middle comes out clean. Liberally brush the top of the cake with rum and dust with caster sugar using a sieve. Leave to cool, then remove the collar and paper. Unlike many fruit cakes this is good eaten straightaway. Wrap in foil or pop into a tin to transport.

Kit Sharp knife

DATE BROWNIES

Having featured brownies in pretty much every single book I have written involving sweet stuff, I wasn't going to include them here. But, when it came to a rushed end of summer picnic, I happened to have some of these in the freezer, and they went down so well I felt they had to be squeezed in, even if it does mean there is now a ridiculous amount of chocolate in this chapter. The dates make the brownies even stickier than usual, well on their way to being a parfait once they are soft.

Makes 1 x 23cm tray of brownies

300g dark chocolate (approx. 50 per cent cocoa solids), broken up
180g lightly salted butter, diced
150g light muscovado sugar
4 medium eggs, and 1 egg yolk
115g ground almonds
100g plain flour
15g cocoa
1 rounded teaspoon baking powder
3 tablespoons strong black coffee
100g dark chocolate (approx. 70 per cent cocoa solids), chopped
100g Medjool dates, halved lengthways, stoned and sliced across
icing sugar, for dusting

Preheat the oven to 150˚C fan/160˚C/gas mark 3. You need a 23cm square brownie tin 4cm deep, or the equivalent in size. Provided it is non-stick there is no need to butter and flour it. Gently melt the 50 per cent cocoa chocolate with the butter in a bowl set over a pan with a little simmering water in it. Remove from the heat, add the sugar and whisk to get rid of any lumps.

Add the eggs and yolk to the chocolate mixture – one by one and beating after each addition, continuing to beat at the end until the mixture is very glossy and amalgamated. Gently fold in the ground almonds, then sift over the flour, cocoa, and baking powder and fold in without overmixing. Stir in the coffee, and fold in two thirds of the chopped chocolate and the dates, separating out the pieces.

Pour the chocolate mixture into the tin and scatter the rest of the chocolate over the top. Bake for 25–30 minutes until the outside of the cake is risen and slighty cracked, a skewer inserted into this section should come out with just a few gooey crumbs, and likewise in the centre. Run a knife around the edge of the tin, and leave the cake to cool, then chill for several hours or overnight. Lightly dust with icing sugar and slice into 25 mini squares.

POLKA DOT COOKIES

You're never too old for Smarties, and these blowsy crisp cookies are sure to brighten any picnic rug.

Makes approx. 10–12 big cookies

125g unsalted butter, diced
75g golden caster sugar
3 tablespoons golden syrup
1 teaspoon vanilla extract
180g plain flour

½ teaspoon baking powder
½ teaspoon bicarbonate of soda
vegetable oil, for brushing
2½ tubes of Smarties

Cream the butter and sugar together in a food-processor until pale and fluffy, then add the golden syrup and vanilla. Sift the flour, baking powder and bicarbonate of soda together, add to the butter and sugar mixture and whizz to a dough, then remove and wrap in clingfilm and chill for at least 30 minutes.

Preheat the oven to 180°C fan/190°C/gas mark 6, and lightly oil two baking sheets.

Form the dough into balls the size of a walnut and gently flatten them between your palms into chubby discs about 5cm in diameter. Arrange these spaced well apart on the baking sheets and bake for 12–14 minutes until evenly golden and slightly risen.

While still warm, press the Smarties into the surface, one in the centre and six around the outside. Leave the cookies for 5 minutes, then loosen them with a palette knife and leave to cool. They keep well for several days in an airtight container. It is a good idea to transport them neatly stacked, if you shake them around, the Smarties are likely to come loose.

SALT CARAMEL MILLIONAIRE'S SHORTBREAD

I can think of several children, forced to name their all-time favourite biscuit or cake, who would without hesitation say 'millionaire's shortbread'. Although not just any old millionaire's, it's got to be homemade. The offer here has the promise of a good chocolate along with a caramel with a hint of salt. The white chocolate marbling is pretty, though not essential.

Makes 1 x 23cm square tin

Shortbread
225g unsalted butter, chilled and diced
100g golden caster sugar
200g plain flour
115g ground almonds
1 teaspoon vanilla extract

Caramel
100g unsalted butter
70g golden caster sugar
1 tablespoon golden syrup
275g dulce de leche (or Nestlé's Caramel Carnation)
1/3 level teaspoon fine sea salt

Top
200g dark chocolate (approx. 50 per cent cocoa solids), broken into pieces
25g white chocolate chips (optional)

Place all the ingredients for the shortbread in a food-processor and whizz to a dough. Butter a 27cm x 18cm or 23cm square brownie tin and press the shortbread into the base, you can lay a sheet of clingfilm over the top to help smooth it. Prick with a fork, loosely cover with clingfilm and chill for at least 1 hour.

Preheat the oven to 140°C fan/150°C/gas mark 2 and bake the shortbread straight from the fridge for 45 minutes until very lightly coloured, then leave it to cool.

Place all the ingredients for the caramel in a small non-stick saucepan and bring to the boil, stirring until melted and amalgamated. Simmer very gently for 8–9 minutes, stirring frequently, then pour over the shortbread base and leave to cool for at least an hour until set, overnight is even better.

Melt the dark chocolate in a bowl set over a pan with a little simmering water in it, and smooth in a thin layer over the top of the caramel. If you want to marble the surface, then melt the white chocolate in the same way, and drop ¼ teaspoons on top of the dark, and marble it by swirling with a cocktail stick or the top of a metal skewer. You have to work quite quickly here – if, for any reason, the dark chocolate starts to set, then you can pop it momentarily into a low oven until it softens again.

Set aside in a cool place until set but still soft, then cut into squares (a small serrated knife is best for this) and leave to set completely in a cool place, then chill. This sweet offering will keep well in a covered container for several days somewhere cool.

Kit Sharp knife

MELTING MOMENTS

Piled high on a plate, these little cakes are worthy of a place at the Mad Hatter's tea party in *Alice's Adventures in Wonderland*. It's basically a type of shortbread that is true to its name, but with a little jam on top they have cake like appeal. If you want something in a paper case but don't want to rustle up cupcakes then these fit the bill, they're also egg free, so perfect for anyone with an allergy.

Makes 14–17 biscuits

150g unsalted butter, diced
75g icing sugar, sifted
finely grated zest of 1 lemon
25g cornflour, sifted

150g self-raising flour, sifted
1–2 tablespoons seedless raspberry jam
icing sugar, for dusting

Preheat the oven to 170°C fan/180°C/gas mark 5. Cream the butter, sugar and lemon zest together, you can do this in a food-processor, then add the cornflour and flour. You should have a soft squidgy dough.

Arrange about 14 paper cases inside a couple of fairy cake tins. Roll the dough into balls the size of a walnut, and using your finger indent a shallow hole into each one. Place these hole-up in the baking cases, gently pressing them onto the base to steady them. Bake for 15–17 minutes until lightly coloured, then remove and leave them to cool. Note, if you're using two trays the bottom may take a little longer than the top.

Drop a little jam into the middle of each cake to fill the holes, and lightly dust with icing sugar using a tea strainer. Set aside for an hour or two for the jam to set a little. Transport to your picnic on a plate or in a tin. The cakes will keep well for up to a week in a sealed container.

LAVENDER SHORTBREAD

This shortbread derives from Castle Farm in Kent, England, which cultivate swathes of different kinds of lavender. Its slightly astringent perfume makes for a very particular shortbread, here using ground rice, which gives it a lovely grainy finish. As a child I remember ground rice was a regular milky pud on the table along with rice pudding, but these days this ingredient is most likely to be found in the Indian section of any shop. Failing that, you can grind your own using a coffee grinder, in which case the finer the better.

Makes 18 fingers

150g lightly salted butter, softened
75g caster sugar, plus extra for dusting
15 drops lavender essence
150g plain flour
75g ground rice
finely grated zest of 1 lemon
a pinch of dried or fresh lavender flowers, plus
  extra for decorating (optional)

Preheat the oven to 150°C fan/160°C/gas mark 3 and line a 27cm x 18cm baking tin with baking paper, taking it up the sides.

Cream the butter, sugar and lavender essence in a large bowl using an electric whisk, then add the flour, ground rice, lemon zest and lavender flowers and whisk until the mixture is crumbly. Press this into the lined tin, without totally compressing to leave it quite crumbly, and bake for 30–35 minutes until pale gold, then remove and dust with sugar.

Leave to cool and then cut into fingers. You can also scatter over a few more lavender flowers.

BLACK FOREST FRIDGE CAKE

Of all the biscuits that can be used to make a fridge cake, nothing satisfies quite like a digestive – or Sables Anglais L'Original as the French would have it, which gives them a much more glamorous spin. It's that wholesome grainy finish that spars with the silky chocolate surround. Add in juicy glacé cherries and we are deep in the Black Forest country.

Makes 25 squares

300g dark chocolate (approx. 70 per cent cocoa solids), broken into pieces
180g unsalted butter, diced
1½ tablespoons golden syrup

150g raisins
180g glacé cherries, halved
250g digestives, broken into 1–2cm nibs
icing sugar, for dusting

Gently melt the chocolate, butter and syrup in a large bowl set over a pan with a little simmering water in it, stirring until smooth. Stir in the raisins, the cherries and the biscuits, tossing until everything is coated in the chocolate mixture.

Line the base of a 23cm square brownie tin with baking paper (you can dab a little of the melted chocolate mixture on the four corners to make it stick), and spoon the mixture over the base of the tin. Lay a sheet of clingfilm over the surface, and press it level using your hands, though it will still appear slightly craggy. Remove the clingfilm and loosely cover with another sheet of baking paper, then chill for 2–3 hours until hard.

Run a knife around the edge of the tin to remove the slab and lift off the paper. Place upwards on a board and liberally dust with icing sugar using a tea strainer. Cut into whatever size squares you'd like and chill. It will keep well for a good week, but you may want to give it another flurry of icing sugar close to the time of serving. Transport in an airtight container or tin.

TIRAMISU IN A JAR

This is my default posh pud for a picnic, ultimately transportable and chic in a clip-top Le Parfait jar. At your destination, simply spoon it into retro plastic or melamine cups with saucers.

For 4 people

100ml strong black coffee, cooled
50ml Kahlua or Tia Maria
2 medium eggs, separated
50g golden caster sugar
350g mascarpone
1 teaspoon vanilla extract
100–120g sponge fingers
cocoa, for dusting

Combine the coffee and liqueur in a shallow bowl. Whisk the egg whites until they are stiff in a large bowl using an electric whisk, then whisk the yolks and sugar together in another bowl. Beat the mascarpone into the egg yolk mixture until smooth, and then the vanilla, and fold in the egg whites in two goes.

Dip enough sponge fingers to cover the base of a 1-litre jar into the coffee-liqueur mixture until the sponge just starts to yield between your fingers, but not so that it is totally sodden, breaking them to fit as necessary. Spoon about a quarter of the mousse on top, and continue layering until you have used up all the ingredients, ending with mascarpone mousse. You should get about four layers of each. Liberally dust the surface with cocoa, close and chill for at least 2 hours.

Kit Serving spoon, spoons

TOFFEE APPLES

Toffee apples on sticks are one of the ultimately portable sweet treats. Make a box of these to hand round as the finale to a picnic. Small apples intended for children are the ideal size, you don't want anything too hearty. A little cinnamon is always welcome with apples, and it is important to use a refined white caster sugar here, otherwise the colour can be hard to gauge as the caramel darkens. That aside, they are as easy as pie.

Makes 6

6 smallish apples
groundnut oil, for brushing
250g caster sugar
½ teaspoon ground cinnamon

Cut off the stalks from the apples level with the fruit and insert a lolly stick into the top of each one. Brush a baking sheet with oil.

Gently heat the sugar in a medium saucepan until it starts to liquefy. Once about half of it has liquefied and started to colour, you can gently stir it. Keep a careful eye on it, stirring frequently until it is a deep gold.

Remove the pan from the heat and stir in the cinnamon. Dip each apple into the caramel to coat it all over, allowing any excess to trickle back into the pan, and place, base-down, on the oiled baking sheet. The caramel should set hard within a matter of minutes, leave them to cool completely.

CUPCAKE JELLIES

These refreshing little fruit juice jellies, made in coloured silicone muffin moulds, are great with a teatime spread of sandwiches and cake. Eat them with abandon, they're good for you. But you could also take a can of squirty cream.

Makes 12

5 gelatine leaves, cut into broad strips (or 1¼ sachets powdered gelatine, see below)
300ml smooth fresh orange juice

a couple of squeezes of lemon juice
300ml red grape juice

Divide the gelatine leaves equally between two bowls, cover with cold water and leave to soak for 5 minutes, then drain. Pour a tablespoon and a half of boiling water over the gelatine in each bowl and stir until it dissolves.

Spoon about 3 tablespoons of the orange juice one at a time into one of the bowls, then mix this back in with the rest of the orange juice, and add a squeeze of lemon juice. In the other bowl, do the same with the grape juice.

Lay 12 silicone muffin cases out in a roasting or baking dish, fill six with the orange jelly solution, and six with the grape solution. Chill for several hours or overnight until set. Transport in a shallow baking tray.

Powdered Gelatine
Sprinkle the gelatine over a few tablespoons of just-boiled water in a small bowl. Leave it for several minutes to soften, then stir for a minute or two, by which time you should have a clear sticky solution.

If the gelatine hasn't completely dissolved, place the bowl within another bowl of just-boiled water and leave for a few minutes longer, then give it a good stir. Alternatively, pour the mixture into a bowl set over a pan with a little simmering water, as though you were melting chocolate, and gently heat. Divide the mixture between the two bowls and follow the recipe as above.

Kit Spoons

INDEX

A

aioli, cheat's 30

almonds: almond
Madeira 154
financiers 157

anchovies: anchovy
buns 65
egg mayonnaise
saladinis 61
leg of lamb with
anchovies 112
tomato and anchovy
pan bagnat 57

apples: apples with
Cheddar 149
orchard shortcake
pie 153
toffee apples 171

apricots: trifle on a
plate 150

asparagus and smoked
salmon frittata 70

aubergines: aubergine
veggie roast 116
oven-roast
ratatouille 94

B

bacon: lemon chicken
fillets with crispy
bacon 135

baklava 149

bananas: banana fool 150
sun-baked 150

barbecues 16, 130–43

beef: rare roast beef with
balsamic peppers 115
steak with garlic
butter 139

biscuits: Black Forest
fridge cake 168
lavender shortbread 167

melting moments 166
polka dot cookies 163
salt caramel millionaire's
shortbread 164

Black Forest fridge
cake 168

blackberries: orchard
shortcake pie 153

bread 49, 50, 143
bread and cheese 58
bread and
tomatoes 54–7
bruschetta 57
crusty garlic olive
bread 53
pa amb oli 54
tomato and anchovy
pan bagnat 57

broccoli: grilled broccoli
and sesame salad 92

brownies, date 162

bruschetta 57

burgers: basil 134
fondue mushroom 139

butternut squash: spicy
butternut squash
soup 126

C

cabbage: picnic
coleslaw 84

cakes 146
almond Madeira 154
date brownies 162
farmhouse sultana 161

caramel: salt caramel
flapjacks 158
salt caramel millionaire's
shortbread 164

carrots 81
picnic coleslaw 84

cashew nuts: new potato,
roasted red onion and

cashew salad 85

casserole, meatball and
bean 129

celery 81

cheese 50, 149
and onion muffins 65
apples with Cheddar 149
aubergine veggie roast
with goat's cheese and
tomatoes 116
bread and cheese 58
cherry tomato and
Parmesan galettes 75
creamed goat's
cheese 30
dates with
Gorgonzola 149
figs with goat's
cheese 149
fondue mushroom
burgers 139
Manchego with quince
cheese 149
pasta timbale with
leeks and goat's
cheese 71
pears with Parmesan 149
potted smoked salmon
with lemon 38
smoked salmon and
cream cheese rolls 62
traveller's croque
monsieur 131
watermelon with feta 149
see also mascarpone

cherries: all-American
cherry pie 152
Black Forest fridge
cake 168

chicken: butter and
lemon chicken 104
chicken tikka masala 108
garlic and thyme

chicken 104
gorgeously buttery very
French chicken 107
Jean-Christophe's
chicken wings 136
lemon chicken fillets
with crispy bacon 135
my favourite picnic
roast chicken 106
a salt and pepper
bird 104
spicy roast
chicken 104
traybake chicken with
za'atar and
pine nuts 110

chicken livers: farmhouse
chicken liver pâté 37

chickpeas: meatball and
bean casserole 129

chillies: cucumber, chilli
and pumpkin seed
salad 91
oven-baked sweet
tomato and chilli
relish 58

chocolate 149
Black Forest fridge
cake 168
date brownies 162
salt caramel
flapjacks 158
salt caramel millionaire's
shortbread 164
sun-baked
bananas 150
triple chocolate
crispies 158

chorizo: meatball and
bean casserole 129

chutney 50

coffee: tiramisu in a jar 171

coleslaw, picnic 84